Effective Teachers in Secondary Schools

Second Edition

Other titles by Tony Swainston

Effective Teachers in Primary Schools (2nd edition) – Tony Swainston
Effective Leadership in Schools – Tony Swainston
Behaviour Management – Tony Swainston

A refl...
perfo...

Effe... in
Sec...s

Second E...

Tony Sv...

network
continuum

Continuum International Publishing Group
Network Continuum
The Tower Building   80 Maiden Lane, Suite 704
11 York Road   New York,
London   NY 10038
SE1 7NX

www.networkcontinuum.co.uk
www.continuumbooks.com

British Library Cataloguing-in-Publication Data
A catalogue record for this book is available from the British Library.
ISBN: 9781855394634 (paperback)

Library of Congress Cataloging-in-Publication Data
The catalog record for this book is available from the Library of Congress

Typeset by Fakenham Photosetting Limited, Fakenham, Norfolk
Printed and bound in Great Britain by Antony Rowe

Contents

About the author

Tony Swainston taught for 20 years in three comprehensive schools. During this time, as well as being a physics teacher, he had a number of roles including pastoral head of year and assistant headteacher. He completed the National Professional Qualification for Headteachers (NPQH) before working for the Department for Education and Skills and then the TDA (Training and Development Agency for Schools) for three years as a Regional Continuing Professional Development Adviser.

In 2006 he set up his own consultancy, E.C.M. Connections Ltd. The central focus of E.C.M. Connections is that Every Citizen Matters and the core belief is in the tremendous potential of each individual. E.C.M. Connections Ltd works to develop the efficacy of individuals, the collective effectiveness of groups and the culture of whole organizations and communities. (Visit www.ecmconnections.co.uk.)

Through E.C.M. Connections Ltd, Tony is a Regional Continuing Professional Development Adviser for Teachers TV. He is also a Project Director for The Pacific Institute, which focuses on the management of change, effective leadership, setting goals to achieve results, and thinking in ways that create success.

Tony's work in education now includes running leadership training programmes for headteachers and other leaders, effective teacher and behaviour courses for teachers, and coaching throughout a wide spectrum of school staff. He also trains facilitators, who then work with parents through a programme called STEPS.

Tony is a highly sought-after facilitator and speaker. He has spoken internationally to educational leaders in six countries about 'The Teacher as the Lead Learner'.

Tony's wife teaches French and they have three children.

You can contact Tony at tony.swainston@ecmconnections.co.uk.

Acknowledgements

I am eternally grateful to the five teachers in Effective Teachers in Secondary Schools who allowed me to film them in their classrooms. From initial discussions with Gervase Phinn 11 years ago, when he was a Senior Adviser in North Yorkshire, the seed of an idea that developed into the VITAL (Visually Instructive Teaching And Learning) project was planted. I am thankful to Gervase for the encouragement he gave me at that time. Instrumental in the development of the VITAL project have also been John Freeman (a Senior Adviser in Leeds), Chris Edwards (the Chief Executive of Education Leeds), Anne Clarke (headteacher of Benton Park School in Leeds) and Elspeth Jones (Dean at Leeds Metropolitan University). All of these have given me tremendous encouragement and support.

Four people who became good friends carried out the filming and editing of all of the material for the VITAL project: they are Mike Hooper, Andy Riley, Bob Bajorek and Paul Wilmott from Leeds Metropolitan University. Thanks also to John Lynch from Leeds Met for organizing all the filming.

Preface to the new edition

Change and progress

Since I started the Visually Instructive Teaching and Learning (VITAL) project over five years ago, things have changed in the world. I have not been able to maintain contact with all of the teachers filmed for *Effective Teachers in Secondary Schools* and *Effective Teachers in Primary Schools* but, of those whom I am still in touch with, two have become successful headteachers and another is now a deputy headteacher.

Education has gone through many changes as well. The diagram below shows some of the challenges presently facing schools, but these constantly develop, with initiatives being imposed all the time.

There is, in my view, nothing intrinsically wrong with change. It is natural and an essential part of life. Our understanding of the world and the way that we most effectively operate within it is constantly shifting and we need to respond in a proactive way to the changes. Schools have to adapt to embrace new ways of thinking, and to constantly reflect on the main purpose of education and the most appropriate way of responding to this. Teachers I speak to feel, however, that they are often the victims of change, that they are being coerced into change rather than being intrinsically part of the developmental change process. As human beings we do not take well or respond most effectively to being told we have to do something. We will naturally react against this unless we can see the benefit of the change that is taking place, both to ourselves and to the work we are doing. It may be that the government is now aware of this concern in a greater sense than ever before. It says that 'schools are leading the system'. This is the new mantra.

The National Challenges

Present challenges

1. The Five Year Strategy
2. Every Child Matters
3. Schools leading the system
4. Workforce reform
5. Leadership at all levels
6. School improvement
7. Performance management
8. National strategies
9. Personalized learning
10. Assessment for learning
11. Strong moral purpose

It is certainly true that the continuing professional development (CPD) of teachers and all those who work directly with schools is now very much part of the responsibility of schools. Schools now own the CPD budgets, with local authorities (LAs) acting ever more as honest brokers of professional development. The problem is that the perception that many schools, headteachers, teachers and support staff have is that the control still lies outside their own sphere of influence. I now do a lot of work with The Pacific Institute and a programme called Investment in Excellence. In this we talk about 'the locus of control' and where this lies. People can only operate effectively, they can only move towards fulfilling their potential, when they experience the locus of control lying inside of them – in other words, when they feel that they are in control of their own destiny, that they shape their future. Without this they can be either passively or aggressively defensive when change comes along and appears to be imposed upon them. It does not help either when teachers do not regard the things that they are told to concentrate their efforts on the so-called standards, or published results, as the most important part of their work. This is not where teachers in general feel they make the real difference that they so dearly want to make in the precious lives of students. But attainment levels are easily assessed and so we continue to assess them. Was Einstein talking directly about teaching when he said, 'Not everything that can be counted counts, and not everything that counts can be counted'? Probably not, but it certainly seems to fit the way we assess the progress made by students and therefore the pressure it puts on teachers to go along with this. The real joy of teaching lies in the fact that each individual can constantly grow and develop. That includes the personal growth we feel as teachers. This growth and change is something we are in control of. It is the thing that motivates us daily in the work that we do. It sets us a goal that we are inspired to move towards. The vision of being the very best teacher we can be brings energy into all the work that we do. This is why *Effective Teachers in Secondary Schools* is as relevant now as it was when I first embarked on filming teachers, talking to teachers and analysing what makes teachers effective in what they do. As teachers we will always have setbacks. Some days will seem difficult and some students may present challenging hurdles that can seem impossible to get over. This in reality is never the case unless we want to tell ourselves that it is. There is always a way. The 'locus of control' lies with us.

By observing other teachers we can learn. By unpicking the elements of their effective teaching skills and professional characteristics we can reflect on our own practice and in a consciously competent way we move towards an ever greater personal effectiveness. We need to be reflective practitioners because we want to grow and also because we want to help other teachers to grow as classroom practitioners and in all of their interactions with students. This is the way that we can best help to nurture all of the students with whom we are privileged to work (and even those that we may at times not classify this way!).

Teaching can be the best, the most rewarding and the most important job in the world. It can also be an immense challenge. We owe it to ourselves to spend time working on how we can do what we do ever more effectively. It will make our work increasingly enjoyable and less stressful. It will also model to students that we are lifelong learners. It is a voyage of unending discovery that we can all take immense pleasure in being part of. I will finish here with another quotation from Einstein, who this time is talking about the work we do. He said, 'Teaching should be such that what is offered is perceived as a valuable gift and not as a hard duty.'

My hope is that the gift that you offer each day of your teaching life can be enhanced in some small way by the fact that you are reading this book and watching the teachers on the DVDs associated with it.

The thin slice of a teacher

In Malcolm Gladwell's excellent book *Blink*, Gladwell talks about the rapid cognition that we can often experience at times but cannot explain in any very logical way. He refers to this as a 'thin slice'. He says, '"thin-slicing" refers to the ability of our unconscious to find patterns in situations and behaviour based on very narrow slices of experience' (page 23). It is often said that young children, dogs and cats can very rapidly 'know' when a stranger is either friendly or a threat. We say that they instinctively know this. They detect, in some almost apparently mystical way or with some sixth sense, that the stranger before them is to be trusted or, alternatively, may harm them. This has no doubt been a major part of the way that we have evolved as human beings and part of our survival strategy. If, when we lived in caves and hunted in hostile environments, we happened to meet a stranger, we then needed to be quickly aware of the action we had to take. There was no time to conduct a search through criminal files to see whether this person had a record of seeking out hunters, whacking them over the head with a very large piece of wood and running off with their prey. Instead we would make a quick instinctive judgement, and if there was any threat of danger, we would either run away or try to whack them over their head with our own hidden mace before they could attack us. This is what we all know as the 'flight or fight' syndrome.

This 'thin slicing', or taking of a small amount of information to arrive at a judgement, can happen in many ways in our modern life. Malcolm Gladwell gives an example of this. In 1983 the J. Paul Getty Museum was on the point of buying a marble statue apparently dating back to the sixth century BC. The statue, called a kouros (a sculpture of a nude male youth standing with his left leg forward and his arms at his side), was examined by experts. Scientists went to work on it. They used modern-day technology including electron microscopes, mass spectrometry and X-ray diffraction machines to ascertain whether the statue was a fake or was genuinely old. Their verdict was that it was not some contemporary fake. And then Evelyn Harrison, one of the world's foremost experts on Greek sculpture, looked at the statue and through an instinctive sense that something was amiss caused the Getty Museum to question whether they should buy the statue. Why did she feel something was not right? Well, she couldn't say. She just had a hunch. Something about the statue, a thin slice of information that reacted with her subconscious, told her that this was not a genuine sixth-century BC statue. Other art experts looked at the statue and felt a similar 'intuitive repulsion'. Eventually the statue was determined to be a fake made in Rome in the 1980s.

The point of this is that, at times, deep analysis of situations may not reveal the truth any more than what we might initially and instinctively feel. In fact, it can sometimes get in the way. Is this why as adults we may not be as good as young children at determining the friendliness or otherwise of people we meet for the first time? Have we been conditioned to think in such a way that drawing on our logical framework can obscure the truth that would otherwise have been obvious to us? Is it because we would have struggled to articulate what was obvious to us that we start to dismiss these kinds of initial impressions as fanciful when we develop into adulthood?

In this book, and with the aid of the associated DVDs, we will explore the building blocks of what an effective teacher looks like. These building blocks include the teaching skills and professional characteristics, together with the associated classroom climate. The link between this and the concept of the thin slice of a teacher is that the aspects of the effective teacher that we analyse must then become part of what the teacher is about. It is part of the way the teacher is, and not just something that might appear on special occasions (for example, when the headteacher happens to be carrying out an observation). This does not mean that any teacher should display all of the teaching skills and professional characteristics all the time. That would be impossible. Rather, it is that the thin slice of a teacher will reveal the underlying essence of what is needed both to be and to develop further as an effective teacher. The thin slice of a teacher comprises the necessary ingredients (I will refer to them as 'qualities') that nourish the development of effective teaching skills and professional characteristics. So what would the thin slice of an effective teacher actually look like?

Having thought about these qualities since I first wrote *Effective Teachers in Secondary Schools*, and having spent many training sessions with teachers discussing the characteristics of effective teaching, it is ever clearer to me that the thin slice of a teacher should include the following 'qualities'. Where it has been possible, these qualities are referenced to the 'Professional Standards for Teachers' and the particular standard given in brackets. So, for example, C1 refers to the 'Core' Professional Standard for Teachers, which states that a teacher should 'have high expectations of children and young people including a commitment to ensuring that they can achieve their full educational potential and to establishing fair, respectful, trusting, supportive and constructive relationships with them'.

Thin Slice 1: A belief in the potential of students (high expectations) (C1)

Students will live up to the expectations that adults and others around them have of them. People may argue about the amount of potential we each have and how much of this we generally use. What is probably less in dispute is the capacity each of us has to achieve greater success in whatever we are doing than we may at present be achieving. This is of course the case with students as well. Successful teachers stretch and challenge students by setting them meaningful and achievable goals.

> The dream begins with a teacher who believes in you, who tugs and pushes and leads you to the next plateau, sometimes poking you with a sharp stick called 'truth'.
>
> *Dan Rather*

Thin Slice 2: Model good manners, positive values and considerate behaviour (C2)

If we are to expect these things from students, then we have got to model this with them. This is a way of demonstrating respect, and students want this as much as adults do. Teachers do this through the very high standards they expect of themselves. If we can hold on to this when we are being severely challenged by students, then we can ultimately expect respect in return.

> The secret of education lies in respecting the pupil.
>
> *Ralph Waldo Emerson*

Thin Slice 3: A sense of humour

Humour can be very important to an effective teacher. This is not about belly-laughing stand-up comedian hysterical stuff, but rather a gentle seam of light-heartedness that teachers bring to teaching and learning. It can create meaningful relationships with a mutual understanding that the stimulating nature of learning is a thoroughly enjoyable experience. Humour allows us to connect with each other as human beings; it can diffuse tension and it lifts our spirits.

Thin Slice 4: Sincerity of intention

No matter what words we speak to students, if they do not sense that our actions match them then they will not believe what we are saying. They will sense that our behaviours do not match. We are saying one thing but our actions (speaking louder than words) are telling them something else. Effective teachers demonstrate that they believe in what they are doing and saying. If we don't do this, then students will very quickly thin slice this particular aspect of us and sense that there is dissonance in our communication.

> *The teacher who is indeed wise does not bid you to enter the house of his wisdom but rather leads you to the threshold of your mind.*
>
> *Kahlil Gibran*

Thin Slice 5: A desire to learn and a willingness to experiment and take risks (C8)

Horace Mann said, 'A teacher who is attempting to teach without inspiring the pupil with a desire to learn is hammering on cold iron.' Without demonstrating that as teachers we have a desire to learn, how can we expect such a desire from students? Effective teachers will always be looking for new ways of teaching lessons and in this way demonstrating to students that they are lifelong learners. These need not be massive changes but at times simply adjustments based on reflection and experience.

> *Who dares to teach must never cease to learn.*
>
> *John Cotton Dana*

Along with the desire to learn is the fact that effective teachers are willing to experiment at times. Again, this need not be something earth-shattering and fundamental. It is also clearly not about potentially harming either the education or the safety of students. Rather, experimenting and taking risks can be something that effective teachers build into their daily actions. Teachers TV has produced some excellent videos that can be freely downloaded. In terms of experimenting and taking risks I recommend that you look at Philip Beadle and a video called *Inspirations – A Lesson from the Best*. You can locate this on Teachers TV at http://www.teachers.tv/video/1399.

> *The art of teaching is the art of assisting discovery.*
>
> *Mark Van Doren, American writer and educator, 1894–1972*

Thin Slice 6: The three Ps – Passion, Patience and Positivity (C2)

Effective teachers demonstrate a real enthusiasm for the subject they are teaching. This passion is what many people will recall from their lessons throughout the rest of their lives.

> *The mediocre teacher tells. The good teacher explains. The superior teacher demonstrates. The great teacher inspires.*
>
> *William Arthur Ward*

Teaching can at times be frustrating. Students can be frustrating and demanding. Teachers, together with the students, may at times feel that things are not progressing at the pace they would like. The professional attributes of a teacher can be strained, but effective teachers are able to demonstrate significant patience and positivity. In other words, they display optimism, believing that any setbacks are temporary and can in themselves be used as learning experiences.

> *Where there is much desire to learn, there of necessity will be much arguing, much writing, many opinions; for opinions in good men is but knowledge in the making.*
>
> *John Milton, English poet, 1608–74*

Thin Slice 7: Fairness (C1) (C18) (C19) (C20) (C21)

Students will feel immense satisfaction whenever they perceive that a teacher is treating them fairly. Effective teachers will deal with all students in a similar way irrespective of their background or their past history. Yet similarity does not imply sameness. Students will accept differentiation if they can sense that this is carried out in a fair way.

> *One looks back with appreciation to the brilliant teachers, but with gratitude to those who touched our human feelings. The curriculum is so much necessary raw material, but warmth is the vital element for the growing plant and for the soul of the child.*
>
> *Carl Jung*

Thin Slice 8: Constructive feedback and support (C1)

Students need to be given guidance by a teacher. They can accept correction when it is given in a constructive and supportive way. Associated with this is what is known as the Pygmalion effect, the Rosenthal effect or, more commonly, the 'teacher expectancy effect'. This refers to situations in which students perform better than other students simply because they are expected to do so. The Pygmalion effect requires a student to internalize the expectations of his or her superiors. It is a kind of self-fulfilling prophecy and, in this respect, students with poor expectations internalize their negative label and those with positive labels succeed accordingly.

Thin Slice 9: Empathy and integrity

The teachers whom you will see in the DVD associated with this book all display empathy. They try to see things from the point of view of the students they are teaching. If students sense that this is the case, they will respond favourably towards the teacher. Alongside this quality is integrity. When teachers stick to a clear moral code and behave in a professional manner, then students feel secure and know where they stand. Teachers build their reputation for having integrity over the lifetime of their careers. Effective teachers demonstrate their integrity through what they do and say. Their integrity guides their decisions, which in turn are based on honesty and truth.

> *A teacher is one who makes himself progressively unnecessary.*
>
> *Thomas Carruthers*

The mnemonic below may assist in recalling the thin slice of a teacher. There may be other qualities that you would include in what you see as being the thin slice of an effective teacher. What is interesting, however, is that these qualities are fundamentally about who we are as human beings. Important as it is to develop our skills as classroom practitioners, it is equally important for us to develop these thin-slice 'qualities'. If we feel that we need to develop some of these qualities, then we can make a start and look for ways in which we can move towards making these become part of our character. We need to look for opportunities to practise these; the opportunities are around us each day. It may at first be a challenge, but with practice what at first seemed to be an act will, through repetition, becomes a habit.

> *We are what we repeatedly do. Excellence is therefore not an act but a habit.*
>
> *Aristotle*

> *What the teacher is, is more important than what he teaches.*
>
> *Karl Menninger*

The **B**elief
in **M**odelling
the joy of **L**earning
with **H**umour,
Sincerity,
Passion
and **F**airness
develops **C**onstructive
Empathy and **I**ntegrity

This is the thin slice of an effective teacher.

Using the Professional Standards for Teachers

In 2007 the Training and Development Agency for Schools (TDA) published *Professional Standards for Teachers: Why Sit Still in Your Career?* These standards attempt to give a sense of continuity and progression through the potential stages of a teacher's professional life.

The TDA website says:

> *The standards will help teachers to review their professional practice, inform their career decisions and identify their professional development needs. Where teachers wish to progress to the next career stage, the next level of the framework provides a reference point for all teachers when considering future development.*

The professional standards cover the following career stages:

- **Q** – qualified teacher status
- **C** – core standards for main scale teachers who have successfully completed their induction
- **P** – post-threshold teachers on the upper pay scale
- **E** – excellent teachers
- **A** – advanced skills teachers (ASTs).

The standards are arranged in three interrelated sections:

- professional **attributes**
- professional **knowledge and understanding**
- professional **skills**.

The standards show clearly what is expected at each career stage. Again the TDA website informs us that:

> *[e]ach set of standards builds on the previous set, so that a teacher being considered for the threshold would need to satisfy the threshold standards (**P**) and meet the core standards (**C**); a teacher aspiring to become an excellent teacher would need to satisfy the standards that are specific to that status (**E**) and meet the preceding standards (**C** and **P**); and a teacher aspiring to become an AST [advanced skills teacher] would need to satisfy the standards that are specific to that status (**A**) as well as meeting the preceding standards (**C**, **P** and **E**) – although they can apply for an AST post before going through the threshold.*

The standards should be used as a backdrop to performance management discussions. Teachers' performance should be viewed in relation to their current career stage and the career stage they are approaching. The relevant standards should be looked at as a whole in order to help teachers identify areas of strength and areas for further professional development.

Professional standards provide the backdrop to discussions about performance and future development. The standards define the professional attributes, knowledge, understanding and skills for teachers at each career stage.

How the standards have been developed

The TDA has a role in bringing coherence to the framework of professional and occupational standards for classroom teachers. This has involved a review of standards for qualified teacher status (QTS), induction, threshold and advanced skills teacher, and the development of standards for the excellent teacher scheme.

From September 2005 the TDA conducted consultations online and through national conferences. Over 7,000 people from the profession responded.

How the standards and the Hay McBer analysis of teacher effectiveness compare

When the Hay McBer Report, financed by the Department for Education and Skills (now the Department for Children, Schools and Families), was published in 2000, it set out clearly the aspects of what makes a teacher effective in the classroom. To assist analysis, it divides the observed effectiveness of a teacher into three aspects: teaching skills, professional characteristics and classroom climate. The three aspects of the Professional Standards for Teachers are professional attributes, professional knowledge and understanding, and professional skills. The following table shows the comparison:

Hay McBer	Professional Standards
Teaching skills	Professional attributes
Professional characteristics	Professional knowledge and understanding
Classroom climate	Professional skills

So what is the link between the two? The simple answer to this is that the Professional Standards for Teachers deals with the broad and holistic nature of the role of the teacher as a professional in a school, whereas the Hay McBer Report looks more closely at what the teacher is doing in the classroom that results in their being effective classroom practitioners. The standards cover the role the role the teacher has in the classroom but in addition the role he or she plays in the broader context of a school. These include the themes of developing professional and constructive relationships, working within the law and frameworks, and professional knowledge and understanding. These are all aspects that impact on the effectiveness of the teacher in the classroom but they are not things that can be easily identified and observed in the classroom. The three themes run throughout the professional standards.

In terms of the theme of developing professional and constructive relationships, the TDA says the rationale is as follows:

> *The education and well-being of children and young people increasingly involves groups of teachers, support staff and other professionals working in schools and across a range of children's services to support learners to fulfil their educational potential, develop positive values and attitudes, and become confident, contributing members of society. The learning and development needs of all children and young people are better met when teachers develop constructive, respectful relationships with colleagues, learners and their parents or carers, founded on effective and considered communication, collaboration and high expectations of all.*

In terms of the theme of working within the law, the TDA says the rationale is as follows:

> *Teachers have legal obligations, rights and contractual entitlements as employees to work within the law and frameworks in order to protect and safeguard the rights and well-being of learners and colleagues. Legislation, statutory and non-statutory frameworks exist to ensure not only that all children and young people receive their educational entitlement but also to protect and safeguard their well-being, both in schools and beyond.*

In terms of the theme of frameworks and professional knowledge and understanding, the TDA says the rationale is as follows:

> *All children and young people, irrespective of background and ability, have a right to receive support, guidance and challenge tailored to their specific needs and abilities. Teachers will be more able to respond to the individual needs of learners, enabling them to make better progress, if they have an understanding and knowledge of how attainment can be raised and the many factors that influence children and young people's well-being, development and ability to learn.*

There are, however, clear links between the Hay McBer Report and the standards where the standards are referring directly to the practice of the teacher in the classroom. The Hay McBer Report and the observation forms that are provided in the appendices to this book can therefore be used to carry out classroom observations. The results of these can then be linked to the standards and used to give very detailed professional feedback to teachers, with a common language used that is specific rather than general. This then leads on to meaningful performance management objectives that can be discussed and that relate to classroom effectiveness. The diagram below illustrates this process.

Step 1	Step 2	Step 3	Step 4
Classroom observation using Hay McBer	Relate this to the professional standards	Give teacher feedback	Set meaningful PM objectives

By using the Hay McBer analysis sheets that have been specially designed for *Effective Teachers in Secondary Schools* and for classroom observations, it is therefore possible to acquire detailed material that can then be linked to the professional standards. The DVD resources and analysis within this book provide guidance on how it is possible to match what we may observe in the classroom with the elements of the Hay McBer Report. All the forms at the back of this book can be downloaded in PDF form from Tony Swainston's website — www.ecmconnections.co.uk.

Section 1

The VITAL Project – Visually Instructive Teaching And Learning

'On the threshold of a dream'

All teachers dream of a classroom where they work in harmony with pupils who behave well and are hungry to learn. I believe this is possible if, as teachers, we are all continually learning from the tremendous abilities possessed by effective teachers around us.

This manual and the DVD that accompany it are intended to assist teachers in their movement towards, and ultimately through, the 'threshold of their dream'.

We can all learn to improve and to be more effective as teachers, no matter how proficient and skilled we are already. This is the core belief that runs through VITAL. We are in a profession where we encourage pupils to continually want to improve, and the best way we can do so is to demonstrate that we ourselves believe in continuous development and growth in our work as teachers – that we ourselves embrace the concept of lifelong learning. The Hay McBer Report makes this clear as follows:

> *The commitment of teachers to their own continuing professional development reminds them of what it is like to be a learner, and helps them develop their own skills and characteristics. This helps them to empathise with pupils, and models the importance of continuous lifelong learning.*

Tony Attwood has expressed how the result of a teaching approach which involves a desire for continuous improvement can in the end provide more efficiency and less stress:

> *The issue is rather like learning to swim. It is quite possible to learn to swim, and avoid drowning, without being much good at swimming. Someone who has studied swimming technique, however, might be able to show you how to swim in a much more efficient way – more output for less input. More result for less stress. Even an expert swimmer can improve – can squeeze that extra one hundredth of a second out of a swimming length. The same is true in teaching.*
>
> *Tony Attwood*

Analysis of the teachers draws heavily on the Hay McBer Report, which was released in June 2000. At the moment I believe the Hay McBer Report is a very valuable but underused piece of research. Part of the reason why it has not been extensively used in a lot of schools is down to the lack of time that teachers feel they have for studying reports such as this one. My hope is that the VITAL project will bring the Hay McBer Report to life and demonstrate its real value.

The sections from the lessons you see on the DVD are not set-up situations. Sometimes the classes were not told until immediately before entering the classroom that they were going to be filmed. I wanted to capture as much as possible real-life classroom experiences. It is of course true to say that as soon as you bring another individual (an OFSTED inspector for example!!) into the classroom the children will change and behave differently (and the teacher certainly, in the case of the OFSTED inspector!!). The aim of the DVD, however, is to provide you with examples of real teachers in real lessons who are effective practitioners in the art of teaching and interacting with their classes.

The VITAL project started in my mind some four years ago and developed from my experience over a number of years as a Head of Year. I felt frustrated that I was often dealing with the same problems created by the same pupils in the same classrooms with the same teachers. These pupils were at times not presenting problems to other teachers, and although I often knew instinctively why this was, I never found it easy to know how to suggest effective strategies to my colleagues and friends without it appearing to be patronizing. At the same time, however, I felt it was unfair to leave teachers to struggle with what they saw as difficult pupils. It has to be said that it was not fair at times on the pupil concerned either. I decided then that I would like to study what common characteristics could be uncovered for effective classroom teachers. The best way I thought this could then be shared by others was through filming teachers who demonstrated effective classroom techniques.

The pupils in VITAL may seem to be an unrepresentative sample of consistently 'well behaved' individuals. I can assure you that these are normal pupils and that in different situations if they are bored and don't have the feeling that they are making progress, they appear differently. If you think yourself of different situations where you have been in lectures (first of all, where you have been motivated by the content or presentation, and secondly, where the content and presentation have bored you), you will understand how pupils, like yourself, may react differently in different situations.

No one could claim that the teachers in VITAL can present all the possible ways of dealing with classes. Every teacher is different and indeed this, to me, is what makes teaching, and looking at methods of teaching, so exciting. What I hope you will be able to see, however, are a variety of methods of teaching which are successful, and which other teachers can learn something from.

The five English teachers in VITAL are from four schools in Leeds. As I have said, no one is saying that these teachers cover all the ways in which a teacher can teach effectively. What they do demonstrate, however, is a range of effective strategies that we can all learn something from. Mike Hughes, in his excellent book *Closing the Learning Gap*, said:

> All schools have excellent teachers. More specifically, all schools have teachers who are wonderful exponents of particular aspects of classroom practice, whose expertise should and could be shared with others.
>
> *Mike Hughes*

This is what VITAL aims to do. That is, it provides a convenient vehicle for all teachers to look at and share the expertise of others. Sometimes it is not easy to find the time within the constraints of a normal teaching week to be able to observe colleagues and draw valuable conclusions in a considered way. One of the benefits of VITAL is that it can be used:

- as a mechanism for discussion during school INSET concerning classroom management

- by individual teachers at home who may wish to review their own approach to teaching as all good professionals should do

- by ITT, NQT and GTP students who may wish to supplement their own classroom observation with examples of effective teachers in other schools

- by training colleges and SCITTS who wish to give their classroom students examples of effective teachers and use this as a means of discussion

- by teachers who are reflecting on their classroom teaching practice as the approach to their Threshold application

- by teachers who are reflecting on their classroom teaching practice as they move through the stages of 'performance management'.

More than anything else, my work on the VITAL project has reinforced the already high regard I had for teachers. Like so many teachers who know that they and their colleagues work very hard, I found it extremely annoying when so much of the press we have received is negative and downbeat.

In addition, rewarding as teaching may be – and I believe it is extremely rewarding – being a teacher is nevertheless an extremely exhausting occupation. If nothing else, this alone is surely a good reason for attempting to spread the good practice which exists in schools so that individuals are not working in a vacuum but rather benefiting from the skills, expertise and vast experience of other teachers. This has traditionally been the practice to some extent within subject areas, but not so common within the broader field of looking at general good teaching and learning skills, though this is now changing.

The culture of sharing practice within schools may now be changing for the better, with teaching and learning starting, at last, to take its rightful position as the most important element in the development plan of many schools.

Classroom management and classroom effectiveness is not something that can ever become a precise science. To believe that a formula can be arrived at which will allow teachers to find success in every conceivable situation is, to say the least, very naïve. I firmly believe, however, that we can all learn to be more effective practitioners in the classroom. Unfortunately, this is not, in my experience, a view shared by all teachers. It seems to me that there is a clear dichotomy in the views of teachers, between those who believe that a teacher is either born with the innate skills required to be an effective teacher, or, alternatively, someone who will always struggle; and those who believe, as I do, that the greater part of classroom effectiveness can be learned.

It is perhaps true that individual character plays a significant part in the success of a teacher. The charismatic aspect of the teacher's role in the classroom cannot be denied. At the same time, however, I believe that many of the skills that make a teacher effective can be actively learned. I say 'actively learned' because the alternative is to hope that the skills are somehow stumbled upon by accident or acquired through experience. Some of this undoubtedly happens, but surely, as professionals, it is more advisable that we should not leave it to chance but rather seek to uncover the elements which go to make up an effective classroom practitioner. Knowledge born of experience as distinct from conceptual knowledge is important, but the barriers between practical and theoretical approaches to teaching should be torn down so that all teachers can benefit from the work of all

"Can someone out there ...... Somewhere ... . help me ?"

contributors to the art of teaching. In addition, I would argue that some of what we refer to as the 'natural charisma' of an individual can also be learned by others. Anthony Robbins in his bestselling book *Unlimited Power* makes the argument for developing excellence through modelling very strongly. If we cling on to the view that we are what we are and there is no way to change this, then progress cannot be made. A central theme in VITAL is that by modelling ourselves on effective people we can ourselves become more effective. This is as true in teaching as it is in any other walk of life.

In a report published by the University of London's Institute of Education, Chris Watkins says that 'the classroom is the most complex and least understood situation on the face of the planet'.

This may be stretching it a bit – but not a lot, in my opinion. Again, Chris Watkins says: 'For 60 years studies have shown that the teacher's style of running a group has a major effect on young people's behaviour.' Teachers do make a difference to the education of pupils. It is therefore important that all teachers should strive to be better at the fundamental basis of their work as effective classroom practitioners.

Running an efficient and happy classroom environment is a highly complex skill to master, with studies showing that teachers engage in 1,000 interactions a day – similar to an air-traffic controller. I am convinced that by looking at techniques which are initially unfamiliar to us we may, once we adopt these techniques, eventually claim that they are 'common sense'. As a result, when we have studied classroom effectiveness we may feel that the good practice we encounter we already really knew about in the first place, and that it is indeed just common sense.

What we call common sense only feels natural when it is part of what you do on a regular basis. This is what Stephen R. Covey refers to as a 'habit'. Habits are things that can be good or bad for us. They can be modified or changed, but this is not necessarily easy and may involve a lot of effort to ensure that the habits we wish to maintain are constantly refreshed, and those we wish to get rid of are resisted. Covey says:

> As Horace Mann, the great educator, once said, 'Habits are like a cable. We weave a strand of it every day and soon it cannot be broken.' I personally do not agree with the last part of this expression. I know they can be broken. Habits can be learned and unlearned. But I also know it isn't a quick fix. It involves a process and tremendous commitment.
>
> *Stephen R. Covey*

The best way for something to become a habit is for us to see it in action and then try it out for ourselves. It is important for us to share the wealth of our experience because, as Plautus said:

> *No man is wise enough by himself.*
>
> *Plautus*

The aim of VITAL is to provide material which can be used for observation before it is tried out. Learning is a process of exploration. When an explorer journeys to a new and initially strange land, it takes a while before she can feel comfortable, settle down, and become familiar with the terrain. After a certain time, however, the new and strange land becomes part of her everyday experience, and in some ways it will feel to the explorer that she has always known this place. So it is with teachers who look at new ways of doing something. To begin with it will seem strange, but after a while it will seem quite natural – it will feel as if it was something you have always done. Education often takes us on a journey where we seem to arrive back where we started – and yet our understanding has improved a great deal. T. S. Eliot expressed this process of looking at ideas and the journey this takes us on, in the following way:

> *We must not cease from exploration. And the end of all our exploring will be to arrive where we began and to know the place for the first time.*
>
> *T. S. Eliot*

May I wish you well on your journey as a teacher who is always seeking to be more effective. I hope that the VITAL project proves to be of help to you in some small or more significant way.

Tony Swainston

Ways of using *Effective Teachers in Secondary Schools*

Effective Teachers in Secondary Schools draws heavily on the findings of *A Model of Teacher Effectiveness. Report by Hay McBer to the Department for Education and Employment – June 2000.* The effectiveness of each of the five teachers on the video is therefore related to the written comments in the Hay McBer Report. A summary of the categories within the Report is given in Section 4.

In Section 5, I will attempt to indicate some of the attributes (I have termed these 'key elements') that I think make each of the teachers effective as classroom practitioners. You may well disagree with me – this is not a bad thing. The very act of analysing the teachers is the most important thing you can do with VITAL. Indeed, you may well believe that attributes I have not included are the most important aspects of individual teachers' performance. In addition to my view of the key elements that make each teacher effective I have made reference to the Hay McBer Report and in particular 'teaching skills' and 'professional characteristics'. (I have illustrated the effectiveness of each teacher through one teaching skill and three professional characteristics.)

The written analysis here and the commentary on the edited DVD are intended to serve and help you. There are different ways in which you may wish to use the information in VITAL:

1. You may wish to look at the near-unedited, approximately 30-minute sections on each of the five teachers and draw your own conclusions first. You may then like to compare your analysis with the things I have highlighted about each teacher.

2. Alternatively, you may wish to look at the edited 20-minute DVD first, then read my comments on the teachers, before finally watching the 30-minute sections and adding your own views on what makes each teacher effective.

VITAL can be used by teachers and lecturers with the following in mind:

▸ teachers in their Initial Teacher Training or GTP year. In this case it can by used by schools with ITT/GTP students, universities training teachers, teacher training colleges and individual ITT/GTP students

▸ teachers wishing to apply to go through the Threshold and looking for ways of demonstrating and improving upon their effectiveness

▸ teachers who wish to reflect on carrying out effective classroom observations as part of the Performance Management process

▸ (most importantly) all teachers who believe they can improve their own personal effectiveness as classroom teachers by observing others

- teachers who wish to analyse the classroom teaching aspects of the new Standards for Classroom Teachers

- teachers who wish to coach other teachers effectively.

If we wish to provide the very best possible education for pupils/students in our schools and colleges, we must all, as teachers, be prepared to continually improve and adopt new methods of teaching and learning. The Hay McBer Report makes this clear:

Effective teachers in the future will need to deal with a climate of continual change.

Schools may wish to use VITAL during INSET days, or individual teachers can view and study VITAL in the comfort of their own homes.

My experience of working on the VITAL project has convinced me that effective teachers are found throughout the whole spectrum of the teaching profession. Again, the Hay McBer Report comes to this conclusion as well:

We found that biometric data (i.e. information about teachers' age and teaching experience, additional responsibilities, qualifications, career history and so on) did not allow us to predict their effectiveness as a teacher. Effective and outstanding teachers came from diverse backgrounds... Effective and outstanding teachers teach in all kinds of schools and school contexts.

Section 3

The ART and the ACT of being a teacher

Central to VITAL is the belief that all teachers should view their work in the classroom as an act that can be continuously improved upon. After a while the act will be fully integrated into the personality of the teacher – it will become a habit which feels totally natural. This chapter will look at the ways in which the art and act of teaching can be approached as a lifelong learning process in which the skills we employ can be continuously refined. In *Bridging the Learning Gap* Mike Hughes expresses the ongoing process of learning of a teacher as follows: 'It is a journey that will never end, because, no matter how effective a teacher, department or school, they can always improve.'

We can all learn and improve

The teachers on the DVD know that they have set themselves up potentially to be shot down by other teachers watching them. The cry of 'I don't think he/she is that good' is something they are all aware may happen. None of the teachers on the DVD, however, claims to have learned all there is to know about classroom techniques. One of the great thrills about teaching is that we can always learn more – new ideas, new strategies and new techniques. The variety of styles they employ is testimony to the fact that there is a range of approaches which teachers can employ to achieve success. My discussions with hundreds of teachers have revealed to me how they all believe they are like students continuously learning and developing. What I can tell you is that all teachers who feel like this are effective classroom teachers who are achieving very good results with their pupils.

The easiest thing we can do is to find fault with things – and given half a chance we are all experts at this. I have set out with the aim of showing only positive aspects of teaching, and indeed this is what I believe VITAL does. I have no doubt that if you wished to, it would not be difficult to find fault with the teachers in VITAL. I would ask you to hold back from this, however, because I don't think it will achieve a great deal. It is far better to look for the positive in what they do and learn from this. Henry Ford said:

> *Don't find fault, find a remedy.*
>
> *Henry Ford*

In the context of teaching and *Effective Teachers in Secondary Schools* I want this to mean that the teachers on the DVD should be used to find positive aspects of teaching and that these should be used for our own good – to find our own remedies.

The idea of learning by modelling our teaching performance on that of effective teachers is central to the VITAL project. By modelling other teachers we can learn in weeks what it would otherwise take us years (if ever) to learn. In a sense we model ourselves on others all the time without being aware of it. We should, however, make modelling of others a more systematic process. What you yourself perceive to be the value or otherwise of strategies employed by the teachers in *Effective Teachers in Secondary Schools* depends upon your own ways of viewing these teachers. There is no definitive description of the teachers, or definitive truth about what they do, which will suit everyone. Einstein realized the limitations of trying to define an ultimate truth about anything:

> *Whoever undertakes to set himself up as a judge in the field of truth and knowledge is shipwrecked by the laughter of the gods.*
>
> *Albert Einstein*

In the Pacific Institute's 'Investment in Excellence' and 'STEPS', programmer Lou Tice says that 'We behave and act in accordance with the truth as we perceive it to be'.

Don't be trapped by limiting beliefs

It is very easy to be drawn into a belief system that says that you cannot improve, pupils are difficult, everything is stacked against you and you are the innocent victim. An alternative is to look for the possibilities which exist, and strive for improvement and success. I believe that this is what all effective teachers do. In my discussions with the teachers filmed for *Effective Teachers in Secondary Schools*, it is clear that they all share an air of optimism and a desire to continuously improve. It is not a bad idea to spend a moment now thinking of five key beliefs about teaching and pupils that may at times have limited your progress, and then to think of another five statements about your personal beliefs which can serve to improve your performance and enjoyment of teaching. I believe it is important for you to derive your own examples here. I have included one limiting belief and one positive belief simply as examples. If these are relevant to you then just keep them; if not, then please ignore them.

Limiting beliefs	Positive beliefs
1. I always have trouble with 9H.	1. I enjoy praising pupils and will do it even more in the future.
2.	2.
3.	3.
4.	4.
5.	5.

What it is important to realize is that your limiting beliefs do not have to remain part of you. You may have believed these things at one time and you may believe them now, but you do not have to continue to see things this way.

The skills of the actor

Some people may believe that acting skills play no part in the effectiveness of a teacher. There is perhaps an understandable concern that if a teacher is acting, then she is not being sincere. Sincerity in a teacher is absolutely crucial – pupils will realize when a teacher is not behaving in a sincere manner. Standing in front of a class of 20 to 30 individuals, who may not always be the most receptive audience you could wish for, is not, however, a natural or everyday occurrence for most people. It is therefore essential that a teacher should be able to perform in an effective manner, such that all of the signals she is giving out indicate an individual who is in control. She must come over as a confident and technically-able performer.

One of the most interesting and unexpected aspects of the work I carried out with VITAL was the repeated comment by teachers on how acting skills should be incorporated into teacher training. This occurred on so many occasions that I decided to contact John Mee from the West Yorkshire Playhouse in Leeds for his comments. Following discussions with John and the teachers filmed for VITAL, it is my firm opinion that acting skills should be directly taught to all teachers so that they can be more effective in the classroom. The use of the voice, body language and positioning for maximum effect in the classroom are all things we would like to believe we could do effectively. Many teachers will do these things very effectively, but generally because they have stumbled on these skills or, less likely, because they happen to have been involved in drama training at some stage. It seems to me illogical that such powerful skills should not be taught to all teachers.

Aristotle said:

> *We are what we repeatedly do. Excellence, then, is not an act, but a habit.*
>
> *Aristotle*

By learning acting skills, and also by copying the skills of effective classroom teachers, which we can do by watching the teachers in the VITAL videos, we can all improve our performance. Once we have then practised these skills on a number of occasions, they will become part of us. They become a habit and part of our character. The belief that teachers can improve by observing and modelling themselves on others is a critical element in the final outcome. In the end, as Anthony Robbins quotes, and as the old saying expresses it:

> *Whether you believe you can do something or you believe you can't, you are right.*
>
> *Anthony Robbins*

The confidence and belief system that can develop in a teacher when certain skills are learned was emphasized in the Hay McBer Report, which said that:

> *Effective teachers believe in themselves... Effective teachers see themselves as, and act as, 'leading professionals'.*

It is very important that we all act in certain ways that make our overall performance as effective as possible. Constantly looking at what we do and how we might be able to improve our performance will, at the very least, enable us to meet the new challenges which we will inevitably face as society changes. At the same time I believe it will allow us to constantly look afresh at our classroom interactions, and as a result bring us greater enjoyment, fulfilment and success.

In *The Art of Happiness*, Howard Cutler says:

> *'... there is a reciprocal relationship between a supple mind and the ability to shift perspective: a supple, flexible mind helps us address our problems from a variety of perspectives'.*

Perhaps one of the key things we as teachers need to have is a supple, flexible mind in order that we are always open and receptive to ideas which can affect our lives as teachers. No matter how good an individual teacher may be, there is no doubt that in some aspect they could improve. A great way to improve is to copy the excellence of others. VITAL is one way of allowing us to do this.

Tony Attwood has referred to the benefits of adopting a positive body language, in terms of both the improved effectiveness that this brings in the classroom and, as a spin-off directly related to it, a reduction in stress for the teacher: 'Our view is that adopting positive body language is such an obvious benefit to everyone in education that it is surprising that more people do not pay attention to it. Indeed it is more than likely that a teacher who has taken a small amount of time to study body language could be two or three times more effective in the classroom than a teacher who has just used the body language that he or she has picked up day by day through life. What is more, good and positive body language actually can make you feel a lot less stressed and a lot healthier.'

..... and so finally John ...... in conclusion ...... I'm telling you ..... we really are going to have a good lesson together today!

I am sure that all teachers would welcome any approach which could result in less stress. We can not expect this to happen, however, without there being a conscious effort to look at and copy certain aspects of effective body language. Again, Tony Attwood says: 'But remember, if you make body language just something of slight interest, you won't ever change. You really have to be determined to alter practices you have developed after years of habit'.

VITAL can provide a starting point for this. We can look at the body language of the teachers in VITAL and emulate it until it becomes quite natural for us. The strange thing about acting out positive behaviours is that they actually make you feel better. We probably all know the experience of talking ourselves into a bad mood: the more we feed ourselves with negative talk, the worse we feel. In a similar way we can influence our mood the other way by thinking positive thoughts and acting positively. Again, Tony Attwood has referred to the specific act of smiling as an example of how deliberate, apparently mechanical acts can influence the way we feel: 'The implication of the research means that if we deliberately impose a false image of smiling upon ourselves, then we will feel better, and our lessons will go better as well.' If we 'act out' being a positive and confident teacher, we begin to feel our confidence and effectiveness grow.

Be your own personal leader

Teaching is a job which demands a great deal of energy, and some teachers may argue that they haven't got the time to continually analyse their performance in the classroom. This is

> You can quickly grasp the important difference between the two if you envision a group of producers cutting their way through the jungle with machetes. They're the producers, the problem solvers. They're cutting through the undergrowth, clearing it out.
>
> The managers are behind them, sharpening their machetes, writing policy and procedure manuals, holding muscle development programs, bringing in improving technologies and setting up working schedules and compensation programs for machete wielders.
>
> The leader is the one who climbs the tallest tree, surveys the entire situation, and yells, 'Wrong jungle!'.
>
> But how do the busy, efficient producers and managers often respond? 'Shut up! We're making progress.'
>
> *Stephen R. Covey*

Effective Teachers in Secondary Schools

analogous to the lumberjack desperately trying to cut down trees with a blunt saw. When asked why he didn't stop to sharpen his saw he replied that he didn't have time to do that – he was too busy sawing! Reflection on teaching is important to all of us. Otherwise we may exhaust ourselves doing the job the hard, and perhaps least effective, way when a better solution is just around the corner. Maybe at times (if not all the time) we need to stop being busy, efficient *managers* in our classrooms and try to be our own *personal and effective leaders*. We owe this to ourselves and to the pupils we teach. Stephen R. Covey, in his book *The Seven Habits of Highly Effective People*, gives clarity as to why it is important to have the qualities of leadership as well as management. He draws a distinction between leadership and management as follows:

> *A few moments of reflection can provide a lifetime of benefits. Thinking can develop smarter proactivity and limit time wasted on unnecessary reactivity. Positive thinking expands our zone of used potential. It helps us to focus our efforts on what is essential. There is a great deal of comfort to be had in being seen as a manager – someone who gets things done. And clearly there is a place for being a manager in the role of an effective classroom practitioner. But there is no credit to be had in doing something in a long and less effective way if a better and more efficient solution is available.*

Peter Drucker and Warren Bennis (cited in Stephen R. Corey: *The Seven Habits of Highly Effective People*) said:

> *Management is doing things right; leadership is doing the right things.*
>
> *Peter Drucker and Warren Bennis*

The more time we make available by carrying out tasks as leaders, the more time we have to devote our energies to other tasks essential for effective management in the classroom. In my opinion, teaching is a hard enough job without unnecessarily wearing a hair shirt. Teachers who do this and run around appearing to be constantly busy and stressed may satisfy some inner need they have to appear this way to others, but they may not be best servicing the needs of the pupils they teach. Stephen R. Covey says:

> *'Effectiveness – often even survival – does not depend solely on how much effort we expend, but on whether or not the effort we expend is in the right jungle. And the metamorphosis taking place in every industry and profession demands leadership first and management second.*
>
> *Stephen R. Covey*

We must be aware that we need to rise above the demands of the immediate and, at times, trivia, in order to advance as teachers. This links with the personal time management of a teacher, as referred to in the final paragraphs of this chapter.

We all need to share our vast expertise

The Hay McBer Report highlights the need for teachers to share their good practice. It says:

> *School managers will need to create a school climate that fosters a framework for continuous improvement. One critical dimension is likely to be openness to the integration of good practice from other teachers, regions or even countries.*

Sharing good practice is what VITAL is all about. *Effective Teachers in Secondary Schools* aims to share some of the characteristics of effective teachers.

There is good practice in every school. *Effective Teachers in Secondary Schools* shows a number of effective teachers in action. My hope is that all teachers who look at this DVD will be able to learn something from what they see and that this may act as a catalyst for further mutual sharing of good practice. The DVD can be viewed in the comfort of your own home away from the immediate pressures of school or in the context of organized training sessions concerning effective teaching and learning good practice. It can then be used as a resource that, ideally, will promote open discussion among colleagues in schools, colleges or raising achievement divisions in LAs.

Small things can be big things

If you feel that you cannot learn to be a better teacher, then VITAL is not for you. On the other hand, there may be something, however apparently small, which could have a positive effect on your teaching. Throughout my own 18 years as a teacher I have become increasingly aware of how the sometimes simple things I can do (but maybe up until some point in my teaching have not done, for a variety of reasons) can make a tremendous difference to my teaching. The 'That's really good, I wonder why I haven't done that before' syndrome is certainly what I have experienced on a number of occasions. The small things can make a real difference. Bruce Barton expressed this with these words:

> *Sometimes when I consider what tremendous consequences come from little things ... I am tempted to think there are no little things.*
>
> *Bruce Barton*

What many teachers will think of as obvious good practice in their own classrooms can easily be missed by others who have simply not thought about or encountered a particular technique. We simply don't know what we don't know. The same teachers, however, may themselves miss a number of 'obvious good practice' techniques used by others. I believe that any talk about certain aspects of classroom practice being common sense should be viewed with great caution – common sense is only a reality when it is familiar or a habit.

Be proactive and concentrate on the things you can change

Clearly, there are certain things which are beyond the control of the classroom teacher and these do impact on classroom effectiveness. These include:

▸ timetable constraints, with a teacher a nomad in the school, moving from one classroom to another

- the level of technical support provided – for ICT, for example

- general levels of resources in the classroom

- the mood of pupils, caused by the baggage of problems they bring to school with them

- the time of day and the sequence of lessons within which you see your pupils.

If we simply react to these problems, however, and say that there is nothing we can do to rectify potential problems, then we cannot progress. Stephen R. Covey has drawn up a useful table of reactive and proactive words, which we may benefit from considering for a moment.

Reactive language	Proactive language
• There's nothing I can do.	• Let's look at our alternatives.
• That's just the way I am.	• I can choose a different approach.
• He makes me feel so mad.	• I control my own feeling.
• They won't allow that.	• I can create an effective presentation.
• I have to do that.	• I will choose an appropriate response.
• I can't …	• I choose …
• I must …	• I prefer …
• If only …	• I will …

It is a good idea to start using proactive language in general conversation. Linked with this is the way we face inevitable problems and setbacks in our lives as teachers. With regard to this Covey says:

> *It is not what happens to us, but our response to what happens to us that hurts us.*
>
> *Stephen R. Covey*

Teachers can be proactive and adopt a teacher-centred approach that accepts external limiting factors which are beyond their control and then seeks solutions. This is what effective teachers do. The teachers in VITAL do this. Tony Attwood has written that by adopting effective teaching and learning strategies it is possible to improve the grades of pupils by as much as two GCSE grades. If there is truth in this (and I believe there is), then it is surely not an option for any teacher not to analyse what he or she does in the classroom and be open to the challenge of learning new skills. As with all aspects of life, putting a bit of effort into being more proactive can ultimately make our work easier.

> *The point is that although we may feel as if we are doing everything we can, and feel that any other work would be impossible, these feelings may not be a valid measurement of reality. It may be that we could each of us teach more effectively with less effort.*
>
> *Tony Attwood*

Teachers may say, 'Can this be possible? Is it right to think this in teaching? Can this really be good for us?' I am not suggesting that we should put less effort into what we do, but rather that being more proactive liberates us to ensure that the effort we expend is more focused and directed towards really influencing our pupils' progress. Efficiency achieved through being proactive is as valid in teaching as it is in any other walk of life.

Aim to enjoy teaching – it's good for you and good for your pupils

It is vitally important for teachers to continue to enjoy what they do. I believe this is best done by setting personal challenges, whether they are big or small. We all need to feel there is something that we can aim for – a personal 'goal', if you like. Recently a programme on the BBC looked at what made people happy, and specifically looked at very wealthy people – some, in fact, who had recently won the National Lottery. A lady on the programme said that she had felt very depressed with the amount of wealth she had until she found a challenge. The challenge she found was simply to try to help people. By giving to others she found that she was able to see great purpose in her life. This is of course a very well accepted idea – and one which forms a central part of many religions. A lot of teachers express the idea that a great part of the attraction of teaching is the sense that it is a caring profession, coupled with the feeling of giving pupils something that is of great importance in their life. It is only possible to really give a great deal, however, when one is feeling mentally and physically fit. In the case of teaching this doesn't imply that we all have to be like top-class athletes, but rather, invigorated by the experience of teaching. The aim should be to find as much enjoyment in teaching as in the things we do in our spare time. I know that to some teachers who are feeling particularly stressed this will sound preposterous, but it should be an aim – a powerfully imagined vision or goal – for all of us.

The continuing need for effective teachers will not decrease with modern technology

One thing that struck me while making VITAL was something that may seem quite simple and obvious: that is, how important the role of an effective teacher still is to the good atmosphere in a classroom and the effective progress of pupils. The Hay McBer Report made this clear, and although it may seem obvious (again some would say it is 'common sense'), it needs to be emphasized. There is no doubt that, in the changing world we are entering, information technology will significantly impact on the experience of pupils in schools. As is already happening, the concept of the traditional lesson will change for many pupils, with the techniques for delivery being modified and enhanced. As I watched the VITAL teachers, however, I did question in my own mind how this could ever replace the multisensory experience (the smells, the temperature, the ambience, etc.) that pupils receive in traditional lessons. How could these things ever be easily captured electronically? I don't want to appear to be a Luddite in this respect, because I am very excited by the opportunities for improved learning experiences that ICT offers. Nevertheless, a teacher's ability to effectively communicate, to have the respect of her pupils and to inspire confidence through her enthusiasm will always be a precious commodity. As human beings we all need the personal ingredient provided by interaction with other individuals.

Construct a lesson in the correct way

To a certain extent an analogy can be drawn between teaching and cooking. Just as it is important in cooking to have the right ingredients, to use the right amount of each of them, and to use them in the correct order, so in teaching – the things we do in the classroom, the amount of each thing we do, and the order in which we do them are significant for an effective learning environment. An effective teacher often struggles to explain what he does to make his lessons effective, just as a cook who instinctively knows what to do may struggle to say precisely how he creates a gourmet masterpiece. In teaching, this must be something that is overcome if we wish to be effective coaches. We must strive to become consciously competent about what we do so that all teachers can begin to use the same language to describe the factors that make up an effective teacher. What we do know is that when a teacher uses the right ingredients in a lesson but in the wrong order or in the wrong quantities, the result will always be disappointing.

In VITAL you need to decide what you think is important to you and throw away anything which you think wouldn't work for you. My only request would be for you to give things a go before you discard them – you never know, one of these things might just be an important classroom tool which proves to be very useful.

The quality of a teacher's performance is the quality of their communication

... the quality of your life is the quality of your communication.

Anthony Robbins

If this is true, then the importance of being a good communicator cannot be more important in any walk of life than in teaching. John Freeman, the adviser I have worked closely with on this project, says that most teachers tend to do too much talking in their lessons. It is therefore essential that what we do say is carefully considered. Again, Anthony Robbins believes that a key skill of highly successful people is their ability to create rapport. It is not necessary to have a natural gift in order to do this. What is important is to listen to what pupils say and watch what they do in order to enter into a sense of rapport. This is not to say that we should behave like children but, rather, respond to the ways they view life and therefore learning. Pupils often have a completely different view of life to a teacher and therefore find it hard to respond to the slant on life that the teacher represents to them. Good teachers can empathize to some extent with the views of pupils in order to engage them fully in the work they are doing.

Focus on success

All theories in education, of course, need to be balanced against the reality of life in the classroom. Anyone who has ever taught knows this. It can drain, tire and, at times, emotionally strain every nerve fibre in your body. As teachers we sometimes torture ourselves with dark thoughts and reflections on the failure of one lesson, even when this was in the middle of a series of other highly effective lessons. We tend then to question our skill as a teacher, and if this develops into a circle of persistent worry, it can be highly destructive. VITAL is about reflecting on what we do, but with the aim of improving, which includes looking at what we do well. We must always remember and applaud ourselves for our successes.

Recently Sue Cowley, author of *Starting Teaching: How to Succeed and Survive*, said:

> *Finally, a tip for when you're tearing your hair out and everything is going wrong. Take a step back, and react from your head instead of your heart. Don't respond to poor behaviour emotionally, by blaming yourself and becoming stressed. Instead, view the situation intellectually. Even the most experienced teacher finds some students and some classes hard to deal with.*
>
> *Sue Cowley*

Tomorrow really is another day!

Most teachers are over-critical of themselves. They tend to dwell on examples of less effective lessons and forget the successes they have experienced. I suspect all teachers have experienced this; I certainly have. The reality is that when you wake up the following day the failures of yesterday can be replaced by great successes. We should all perhaps take on board the simple philosophy of Margaret Mitchell in *Gone with the Wind*, who said in 1936, 'After all, tomorrow is another day.' I certainly had to remind myself of this continually when I was teaching.

And just as we, as teachers, feel the great need to experience success, so, clearly, do pupils. Thomas Wolfe once said:

> *There is nothing in the world that takes the chip off one's shoulder like the feeling of success.*
>
> *Thomas Wolfe*

Any teacher will echo this; and it also applies to pupils. When pupils who are used to being given feedback of failure receive a sense of success, their whole persona suddenly changes. They are lifted, they are rejuvenated, and they are suddenly filled with optimism.

Effective Teachers in Secondary Schools

The chip on their shoulder is suddenly removed. This is why giving sincere praise and positive feedback to pupils is so necessary. Some people have said that any negative comment ought to be balanced by at least five positives. This is a good starting point on the learning curve to giving positive feedback as a teacher. Eventually, however, praise will become the norm. This is not to say that pupils should not be told when they do things that are inappropriate. This is, in fact, essential. What is important, however, is to have a general classroom atmosphere that is positive, constructive and imbued with growth.

As I have suggested, it is my belief that we must always strive to improve – there is always something new to be learned. As long as this is the case we should not punish ourselves when things don't go as well as we would have liked. It is vital that we always remember our successes, while being prepared to think and try to correct any difficulties encountered. The very act of thinking is not always easy. But thinking is essential if we are to appreciate fully what we have achieved, what we are successful at, and what we need to work on to improve. Henry Ford expressed the problem people have with thinking:

> *Thinking is the hardest work there is, which is the probable reason why so few engage in it.*
>
> *Henry Ford*

As teachers, it is essential that we think and review our performance on a regular basis.

Believe in yourself

Emerson said:

> *What you are shouts so loudly in my ears I cannot hear what you say.*
>
> *Ralph Waldo Emerson*

To be aware of this is so important for us as teachers. Children all have PhDs in psychology, and will determine immediately the intentions of a teacher. 'Is he fair?' 'Is she firm?' 'Can I trust her?' 'Does he want the best from me?' All these things children will form views on very quickly. If a teacher's intention is not right, they will detect this immediately. (I talk further about this when discussing the 'thin slice' of a teacher.)

Sometimes when a class or pupil is causing a teacher problems, a conscious paradigm shift is of great benefit. Simply constantly holding a paradigm (or a belief or perception) of a class or a pupil as a problem often makes a teacher enter the class with the wrong intention. We have all been there and done that. The trouble is that the class or pupil will then sense that you expect them to misbehave, and the dance will then begin, with both the teacher and the class/pupil knowing the sequence of steps that will follow.

Research apparently shows that people who are effective in whatever walk of life are able to visualize and feel what they are going to do before they do it. I have heard Sally Gunnell say that she pictured precisely how she would run the 400m hurdles race before she set out. It is important for teachers to visualize success in the classroom. If you see yourself as having problems, you will have problems. If you struggle with a positive visualization of yourself in the classroom, then watch the teachers in VITAL, adopt some of their tactics and use these as part of your personal positive visualization. Practising some of the things the teachers in VITAL do (however apparently trivial to begin with) will seem like an act to begin with. But once they have been tried on a number of occasions and been found to be successful they will be internalized and become a habit. Much of the success of top-class athletes has already been determined in their minds before they start a race.

> *Pupils all have PhDs in psychology. They sense any weaknesses at one hundred paces. This is why we owe it to ourselves to be at least one step ahead.*
>
> *Tony Swainston, 2001*

Effective time management

Stephen R. Covey gives a matrix which I have found useful as a way of looking at effective time management. Essentially he defines activities as:

PHds in Innocence Studies and Applied Analysis of Teacher Control Susceptibility

A important and urgent

B important but not urgent

C not important but urgent

D not important and not urgent

Urgent issues are things we feel we must do, or, very often, things that other people try to persuade us that we must do! Certainly other people are often happy to see us do these things. They can also be fairly pleasant, easy or rather mechanical tasks to accomplish but not always important. So what is meant by 'important'?

Important issues are those things which, when accomplished, can have long-term benefits and contribute to your personal mission or the mission of the school. They match your deep values and the goals you have set yourself.

Looking at the matrix overleaf, Covey says that we often focus too much on the Segment A activities. He terms these 'crisis' activities. We can spend so much time on these activities that we find that when we are not doing them, we often escape into Segment D activities as a means of escape.

Some people spend a lot of time carrying out Segment C activities, thinking they are actually carrying out Segment A activities. They are often driven by the requirements of others and think that the things they are doing are important, when in reality there could be a far better way of completing this work – if indeed it needs doing.

The thing we should aim to do is to enter into Segment B activities as much as we can. These are the activities that nurture us and can have a long-term benefit for us, as well as our role as classroom practitioners. Some teachers will argue that they don't have enough time to enter this zone. But the alternative is to be driven by circumstances rather than looking to the opportunities that exist. The choice is between:

A being reactive and being driven by external influences; and

B being proactive and looking to shape what the future will look like.

I am aware that there is value to be had from Segment D ('not important and not urgent' zone). As it says in this segment, these can be pleasant activities – and what is wrong with that? Nothing really, as long as there is enough time left to carry out the crucial work in Segment B ('important but not urgent').

What you put in these categories (segments or zones) will be up to you. I know I have discussed, argued, and disagreed to some extent with my wife (who also teaches) on what they should contain.

I have now facilitated effective teacher courses with hundreds of teachers, many of whom have said that a cup of tea in the staff room for them is both 'urgent' and 'important'. If you feel this is the case for you, then that is fine. There are no absolutely right or wrong items that we should put into the different segments. The important thing that we must realize is that we only have a certain amount of time in each day for our work in our school. Allocating time in a way that best benefits what we are trying to achieve is therefore crucial. Perhaps a regular review of our time management matrix is something that should be in our 'important but not urgent' segment.

I have simply put certain things down in the matrix below for your guidance. However, the process of doing this for yourself is, I believe, very important. I would therefore recommend that you fill in your own matrix in the blank table provided opposite.

	URGENT	NOT URGENT
IMPORTANT	**SEGMENT A** • teaching/preparing lessons • essential marking of books • writing reports • parents' evenings • registers • departmental/pastoral meetings • assemblies	**SEGMENT B** • considering new teaching and learning styles • considering new behaviour management techniques • considering rewards and punishments • keeping up to date with new ideas in education
NOT IMPORTANT	**SEGMENT C** • responding immediately to certain requests of pupils and others • some photocopying • reacting to (or 'dealing with') certain aspects of misbehaviour • responding immediately to certain phone calls	**SEGMENT D** • general trivia • time wasters • cup of tea in the staffroom • responding to a minor phone call • some phone calls • pleasant activities

(Adapted from Stephen R. Covey, *The Seven Habits of Highly Effective People*)

My time management matrix

	URGENT	NOT URGENT
IMPORTANT		
NOT IMPORTANT		

You may wish to photocopy the blank table and fill it in for future reference with your own present ideas. It may then be useful to refer back to it periodically to see if you are beginning to spend more time in Sector B ('important but not urgent'). The importance of rising above the immediate to see the long-term goal is well worth while. As Benjamin Disraeli said, 'Little things affect little minds'. You can also use the time management matrix as an effective coaching tool, with colleagues. Why not try using it when you plan certain lessons as well?

We must all try to be teachers who effectively and efficiently deal with the little things which face us in teaching, so that we can spend time concentrating on the things which may not be urgent – but are in the long term critically important.

Final thoughts

With each of the teachers in VITAL I have given my views on what I believe makes them effective teachers. The importance of looking at the teachers on the DVD that accompanies this book is really to come up with your own conclusion and views. You may therefore wish to look at the teachers first and then read my analysis. You may well disagree with a lot, or perhaps all, of what I say. I believe the process of watching and reflecting on the teachers is more important than it is for everyone to reach the same conclusions.

The important thing for teachers is to keep on learning throughout our careers. Teaching should be viewed as a research-based profession – whether the research is on a large or personal, small scale. We can always learn from new ideas – we should always be willing to look, ask questions and learn. The following quotations referring to the theme of continually asking and enquiring may provide you with some inspiration – and you may indeed wish to display some of them around your classroom.

> Anyone who stops learning is old, whether at twenty or eighty.
>
> Henry Ford

> The fool wonders, the wise man asks.
>
> Benjamin Disraeli

> All men by nature desire knowledge.
>
> Aristotle

> I do not think much of a man who does not know more today than he did yesterday.
>
> Abraham Lincoln

> Knowledge is the antidote to fear.
>
> Ralph Waldo Emerson

> *The important thing is not to stop questioning.*
>
> *Albert Einstein*

> *He who asks is a fool for five minutes, but he who does not ask remains a fool for ever.*
>
> *Old Chinese saying*

> *Not to know is bad; not to wish to know is worse.*
>
> *African proverb*

Being proactive allows a person to be efficient, to be in control and to do the job better. A lot of the wasted time and effort caused by continually reacting to situations and crises without a thoroughly analysed understanding of the best way of dealing with them can be removed by being proactive. The time management matrix above is a useful way of analysing your present time allocated to being proactive and, as a result, a useful incentive for consciously thinking about making a shift where necessary.

Good luck – and I hope you enjoy watching the teachers in *Effective Teachers in Secondary Schools* as much as I enjoyed putting this part of the project together.

Section 4

Summary of the Hay McBer Report

A Model of Teacher Effectiveness. Report by Hay McBer to the Department for Education and Employment – June 2000 looks at the effectiveness of teachers by dividing the analysis up into three key elements. These are:

1 Teaching skills

2 Professional characteristics

3 Classroom climate

All of these things are within teachers' control and significantly influence pupil progress.

Teaching skills

The Report subdivides teaching skills into seven categories, as follows:

A High expectations

B Planning

C Methods and strategies

D Pupil management/discipline

E Time and resource management

F Assessment

G Homework

These are similar to the OFSTED inspection headings. In addition to these seven categories, Hay McBer says that teaching skills can be observed in broad terms by:

▸ the way the lesson is structured and flows

▸ the number of pupils on task through the course of the lesson.

Professional Characteristics

The report subdivides Professional Characteristics into five clusters, as follows:

Cluster	Characteristics
A Professionalism	‖ Challenge and support ‖ Confidence ‖ Creating trust ‖ Respect for others
B Thinking	‖ Analytical thinking ‖ Conceptual thinking
C Planning and setting expectations	‖ Drive for improvement ‖ Information seeking ‖ Initiative
D Leading	‖ Flexibility ‖ Holding people accountable ‖ Managing pupils ‖ Passion for learning
E Relating to others	‖ Impact and influence ‖ Teamworking ‖ Understanding others

Referring to the clusters of professional characteristics, the Hay McBer Report says that :

Effective teachers need to have some strengths in each of them.

The report, however, recognizes the distinctive qualities of each teacher, and makes clear that:

Effective teachers show distinctive combinations of characteristics that result in success for their pupils.

All effective teachers achieve success in a unique way with their own individual emphasis on certain professional characteristics more than others.

Classroom Climate

The report sub-divides Classroom Climate into nine dimensions as follows:

A Clarity   Clarity around the purpose of each lesson – how each lesson relates to the broader subject – as well as clarity regarding the aims and objectives of the school.

B Order   Order within the classroom, where discipline, order and civilized behaviour are maintained.

C Standards   A clear set of standards as to how pupils should behave and what each pupil should do and try to achieve, with a clear focus on higher rather than minimum standards.

D Fairness	The degree to which there is an absence of favouritism, and a consistent link between rewards in the classroom and actual performance.
E Participation	The opportunity for pupils to participate actively in the class by discussion, questioning, giving out materials, and other similar activities.
F Support	Pupils should feel emotionally supported in the classroom, so that they are willing to try new things and learn from mistakes.
G Safety	The degree to which the classroom is a safe place, where pupils are not at risk from emotional bullying, or other fear-inducing factors.
H Interest	Pupils should feel that the classroom is an interesting and exciting place to be, where they feel stimulated to learn.
I Environment	Pupils should feel that the classroom is a comfortable, well-organized, clean and attractive physical environment.

The Hay McBer Report says that Teaching Skills and Professional Characteristics are factors that relate to what a teacher brings to the job. A distinction between the two is drawn as follows:

> *Whilst teaching skills can be learned, sustaining these behaviours over the course of a career will depend on the deeper seated nature of professional characteristics.*

The report describes the nature of professional characteristics as follows:

> *Professional characteristics are deep-seated patterns of behaviour which outstanding teachers display more often, in more circumstances and to a greater degree of intensity than effective colleagues. They are how the teacher does the job, and have to do with self-image and values; traits, or the way the teacher habitually approaches situations; and at the deepest level, the motivation that drives performance.*

Classroom Climate is referred to as an output measure: it is what the teacher creates through Teaching skills and Professional characteristics, and it is what influences the pupils to learn.

As I have indicated, the Hay McBer Report comfortingly says that teachers are not clones and that there are a number of ways for a teacher to achieve effectiveness.

> *There is, in other words, a multiplicity of ways in which particular characteristics determine how a teacher chooses which approach to use from a repertoire of established techniques in order to influence how pupils feel.*

This overview of the Hay McBer Report is useful because in each of the analyses of the teachers in VITAL there will be reference to those factors in the report which apply to the observed effectiveness of the teachers. Five of the seven Teaching Skills (excluding only 'Assessment' and 'Homework') are highlighted in the analyses of the VITAL teachers. All five of the 'Professional Characteristics' clusters, and 15 of the 16 associated characteristics, are highlighted. (The only characteristic not linked with one of the VITAL teachers is 'understanding others'.

In the analysis of each teacher, I have not referred to the Classroom Climate dimensions because these are what the Hay McBer Report says result from the teaching skills and professional characteristics. You will no doubt be able to see a number of Classroom Climate dimensions for yourself in each of the lessons shown, if you wish to do this.

The following quote from the report indicates that the time has come for us to look at other teachers and how they create a positive classroom climate, whilst at the same time being open to comments and suggestions about the classroom climate we ourselves create:

> *Despite the demonstrable impact of classroom climate on student motivation and performance, it is rare for British teachers, or teachers in other countries, to receive structured feedback on the climates they help create in their classroom.*

Since the report was written, in 2000, I believe things have improved, with the coaching and mentoring of teachers making a significant difference to the understanding of how we can progress as professionals. *Effective Teachers in Secondary Schools* can support more effective coaching and mentoring, which in turn will impact on the classroom climate. This in turn will improve student motivation, enhance learning and result in greater student achievement.

Effective teachers – happy pupils: analyses of the teachers in *Effective Teachers in Secondary Schools*

In the following I have picked out some of what I have called the *key elements* in the classroom management of each of the five teachers in *Effective Teachers in Secondary Schools*. The key elements are my initial thoughts on what elements contribute to making an effective teacher. Again, as I have said before, you may well consider yourself that there are other key elements more important than those I have chosen. You may also feel that some of the key elements I have identified in one teacher appear in, or are more relevant to, another teacher. This will almost certainly be the case. The process of deciding in your own mind what the 'key elements' are is what is most important in studying the VITAL teachers.

In addition, I have looked at each teacher in terms of the Teaching Skills and Professional Characteristics identified in the Hay McBer Report. Again, you will have your own view on which of the skills and characteristics are most evident in each teacher. What I have presented is more a framework showing examples of key elements, teaching skills or professional characteristics, rather than a complete and definitive set for each teacher. There will also be some overlap between the key elements I have identified and the teaching skills or professional characteristics identified in the Hay McBer report. I have indicated where I think that this is the case.

For each of the five teachers you will see a brief profile, which I hope will place the teaching of each one in a clearer context. In addition, there is an initial summary of the key elements, teaching skills and professional characteristics identified for each teacher.

Larraine Biscombe

 ...I give 100% to the pupils and I demand 100% from them ... Preparation is the be-all and end-all.

Larraine Biscombe

Larraine Biscombe – VITAL Teacher Profile

Age when filmed:	51
School:	John Smeaton Community High
Number of pupils in the school:	Approximately 1,600
Age range:	11 to 18
Age range Larraine teaches:	11 to 16
Date she joined this school:	1992
Total years of teaching:	25
Previous schools:	Fir Tree Junior School Fir Tree Middle School Various schools on supply during time out from full-time teaching to raise a family!
Subjects taught on the DVD:	French PSHE
Year group taught on the VITAL DVD	Year 8

Larraine Biscombe – Key Elements

These are my initial ideas on some of the characteristics that make Lorraine an effective teacher:

1 pupils immediately on task

2 positive body language

3 earning the respect of pupils

4 assertive use of the voice

5 the importance of the classroom environment

6 having a sense of humour

7 adopting a businesslike approach with high expectations

8 using games and having fun

9 pupil movement

10 personal impact and presence.

Key Element 1 – Pupils immediately on task

The start of a lesson is a critical time in setting the tone for the work to be done. As soon as the pupils begin to enter Larraine's classroom they are on task in French. The period when pupils enter a classroom can present difficulties for a teacher. No one wants to begin a lesson by shouting at a class to be quiet, but this can happen if a class enters the room continuing their discussions from earlier on. Larraine's solution to this is to accept that pupils like to talk (to fill the silence vacuum!) and to use this to her advantage by getting them to chant numbers, dates, etc. as they enter the room and also during transitions between one activity and another.

There is often a period of dead time when pupils enter a classroom. It is, therefore, well worthwhile for a teacher to think about how to make this time more productive, and as a result start the lesson in a more efficient way. This will clearly not involve pupils chanting out numbers in every lesson – this particular technique to get the pupils quickly on task may not suit everyone's style. Simple things like having an instruction written on the board as they enter the classroom, which immediately gives the pupils a task to carry out, is often enough to transform a lesson.

Larraine also has a general policy of the pupils not taking out their books, pens, pencils, etc. at the start of a lesson. Her reason for this is that she believes this exercise can cause a lot of disruption so she prefers to get the class settled and go through the initial part of the lesson without the pupils needing to write anything down.

Q1. **Instant activity**. What techniques do you employ to ensure that pupils are immediately on task as they enter the classroom?

Key Element 2 – Positive body language

Larraine's body language says, without any need for words, 'I am in control, trust me'. The classroom is her domain. She walks around to all quarters of it – no place is in any way a no-go area. She shows great confidence in her interactions with the pupils, inviting them to come out to the front with her, for example, without there being any hint of silliness. Larraine uses skills she says she has learned from acting – but these have now become part of her natural repertoire. What was once an act is now a habit. Repeating a central theme of VITAL: we can all learn new skills in a similar way by mirroring or copying other teachers.

Q2. **Body language**, Have you ever practised your body language by looking in a mirror? Do you have a positive image of how you would like students to see you?

Key Element 3 – Earning the respect of pupils

Larraine's pupils clearly have a deep respect for her. As well as this being obvious from the filmed material, I have witnessed it from walking around the school with Larraine on a number of occasions. She has built up a reputation over a number of years and pupils now know what to expect from her. This is not to say that she ever relaxes in her endeavour to maintain or improve on her standards. When a teacher starts to think she knows all there is to know, and therefore stops trying out new methods in the classroom, this is often the start of a decline in her effectiveness and the standards of teaching, learning and discipline that pupils experience.

Q3. **Earned respect**. Can you name five elements of how you behave in school that earn you the respect of students?

Key Element 4 – Assertive use of the voice

When Larraine gives an instruction there is no doubt in her voice that she expects instant action. She has a very assertive manner which is simultaneously expressive and warm. Again, Larraine has learned to use her voice partly through her interest in acting skills. An understanding of the use of the voice is a critical element in acting skills, which I believe could very productively be used by teachers.

Q4. **Voice**. Are you conscious of how you speak? Are there ways – volume, tone, pace, pauses, for example – that you could experiment with?

Key Element 5 – The importance of the classroom environment

Larraine's room is full of displays of pupils' work and creations of her own. She has taken time over this and the pupils will immediately be aware that she cares about what she does. Caring is very important. It is inevitable that pupils themselves will not care about their work if the teacher appears to lack motivation and interest in teaching them.

Q5. **Classroom environment**. Are there examples on your classroom wall of students' work? Do you change these regularly?

Key Element 6 – A sense of humour

During the lesson, the class laughs along with Larraine. This is a great way of building up relationships. It is important that pupils see that their teacher has a sense of humour, as

Larraine says in her interview. Laughter is a basic way in which all human beings interact and an excellent way of breaking the ice or eliminating tension.

Q6. **Humour**. Do you find that humour is something you employ within the classroom? If not, it is sometimes worthwhile seeing how another teacher does this and trying to copy their style.

Key Element 7 – Adopting a businesslike approach with high expectations

Larraine demands a lot of her pupils in return for the time and effort she puts in. This creates an atmosphere where learning is seen as important and where a structured, businesslike ethos prevails. This is no accident. Larraine plans her lessons with great care, from the structure of the work to be done and materials to be used, to the clothes she wears. This all results in an environment which is safe and peaceful while at the same time being conducive to effective learning. (Mentioning clothes may seem strange in terms of planning a lesson, but pupils pick up an impression through all their senses, and the image the teacher presents in terms of dress will undoubtedly influence their approach to the lesson. The semiotics, or signs and symbols, including the light level, the smell and the acoustics of a classroom which combine to influence the work of pupils, is worth some thought.)

Q7. **A businesslike approach**. Do you adopt a friendly but businesslike approach to teaching so that students are aware of the professional way you are approaching the lesson?

Key Element 8 – Using games and having fun

Teaching should be fun! Robert Powell spends some time in his videos on *Whole Class Teaching* on the use of games, and how they can motivate pupils. Often when pupils are playing games they don't think they are working. Larriane uses card games, which the pupils are clearly actively involved in. They have fun and there is the added ingredient of looking to see who wins, which gives spice to the whole process and is a natural incentive for competitive youngsters.

Q8. **Games**. Do you use games within your lessons? If not, would this be worth experimenting with?

Key Element 9 – Pupil movement

The pupils move around the classroom without any fuss. This is due to the way in which they have realized Larraine's expectations over a period of time. Again, no success comes by accident. Larraine deals with her pupils with a firm but fair manner which allows them to understand the expectations she has, and allows her to be confident in them and trust their behaviour and response to her. Once this process is started it will tend to develop with both teacher and pupils feeling nourished by the relationship which is developing.

Q9. **Kinesthetic activities**. Are kinesthetic activities built into your lesson plans?

Key Element 10 – Personal impact and presence

This attribute is mentioned in the DfEE document *National Standards for Headteachers*, which says that it is possessed and displayed by all successful and effective teachers.

As I have indicated here, Larraine makes a real personal impact in the classroom. Her significant presence operates to get the best from the pupils. Could all teachers learn to be like this? Well, I clearly believe that it is possible and this is a key part of VITAL. But desire is not enough – it does take effort, commitment and time.

Q10. **Impact**. What do you think students would see as being the 'thin slice' of you as a teacher?

Larraine Biscombe – direct links with the Hay McBer Report

The following describes the links I have made between Larraine's teaching and the Hay McBer Report. As for all the teachers I have chosen one Teaching Skill and three Professional Characteristics.

Teaching Skill

The Teaching Skill from the Hay McBer report that I have chosen to Larraine with is:

  C Methods and strategies.

Two of eight key questions the Hay McBer Report asks about 'methods and strategies' are:

> ▸ *Does the teacher involve all pupils in the lesson?*
>
> ▸ *Does the teacher use a variety of activities/learning methods?*

It is evident from the DVD footage that Larraine does both of these things. She uses a variety of question-and-answer techniques, she allows pupils to work through problems together on a variety of exercises, and she listens and responds to the questions of all her pupils. The Hay McBer Report 'saw effective teachers doing a great deal of direct instruction to whole classes, interspersed with individual and small group work'. That is what we see Larraine doing.

Professional characteristics

The three professional characteristics that I have chosen to link with Larraine from the Hay McBer Report are:

Cluster	Characteristics
A Professionalism	**II** Confidence
C Planning and setting expectations	**II** Initiative
D Leading	**II** Managing pupils

A Professionalism – Confidence

Under Professional Characteristics and within the cluster of **A** Professionalism, the Hay McBer Report emphasizes the importance of *confidence*:

> *Effective teachers believe in themselves and have the conviction to be ambitious: for the pupils, for the school, and for themselves. Self-confidence is also fundamental to challenging poor performance and bringing about step change. Effective teachers see themselves as, and act as, 'leading professionals'. They have the emotional resilience to deal with challenging pupils, and the stamina necessary for sustained contribution in the classroom. Being confident about personal skills and believing in the value of their work in what they know is a demanding job, helps teachers to have a strong sense of identity, and to set boundaries for themselves so they know what they can and should take on.*

The video of Larraine clearly demonstrates that she has a lot of confidence in front of the class. Her confidence is exemplified by key elements such as:

▸ positive body language

▸ earning the respect of pupils

▸ assertive use of the voice.

As teachers we will all face challenging situations with pupils who test our determination and skill. Referring to this, the Hay McBer Report says about teachers who demonstrate confidence:

> *They have emotional resilience in dealing with challenging pupils and situations. They are able to keep calm.*

C Planning and setting expectations – Initiative

Under Professional Characteristics and within the cluster of **C** Planning and setting expectations the Hay McBer Report emphasizes the importance of *initiative*:

> *In addition to the careful planning of mainstream lessons and programmes of work, effective teachers think ahead. This enriches the curriculum and makes learning relevant and coherent.*
> *Alert, action-oriented teachers stand out, and command respect, with colleagues as well as pupils.*

Larraine has a great presence in the classroom and around the school. She is very willing to take the lead and demonstrate initiative, demanding respect from both her colleagues and pupils. This is demonstrated through key elements such as:

▸ adopting a businesslike approach with high expectations

▸ using games and having fun

D Leading – Managing pupils

Under Professional Characteristics and within the cluster of **D** leading, the Hay McBer Report emphasizes the importance of *managing pupils*:

> *Takes action on behalf of the class. Speaks positively about the class to others and builds up its image. Goes out of his or her way to obtain the extra materials and resources the class, group or team needs: for example, by engaging the support of parents, the community or commercial organizations.*

Larraine has a calm control of the pupils. Managing pupils effectively helps to create the right climate in the classroom and around the school. Larraine motivates every pupil, and gets them to move forward with her. She focuses their attention on the tasks they are required to do and she makes clear the learning objectives. The following key elements contribute to the way Larraine manages pupils:

- positive body language
- the importance of the classroom environment
- having a sense of humour
- pupil movement.

In relation to managing pupils effectively, the Hay McBer Report mentions the need for effective teachers to have what we sometimes refer to as 'eyes in the back of their heads':

> *Pupils in their classes will be aware of the 'lighthouse effect', the habitual scanning by which effective teachers appear to pick up everything that is going on.*

Larraine demonstrates a great awareness of all that is going on in the classroom, even when groups are involved in very different group exercises at different stages of completion. She also gives very clear directions, gets all pupils quickly on task, and makes learning objectives very transparent to the class at all times, and particularly at the start and end of the lesson. The report refers to this as follows:

> *They get pupils on task, clearly setting learning objectives at the beginning of a lesson and recapping at the end, and giving clear instructions about tasks.*

Les Taggart

They have got to learn by trying things ... that I don't have all the answers.

Les Taggart

Les Taggart – VITAL Teacher profile

Age when filmed:	47
School:	Benton Park School in Leeds
Number of pupils in the school:	Approximately 1,400
Age range:	11 to 18
Age range Les teaches:	11 to 18
Date he joined this school:	1975
Total years of teaching:	26
Previous schools:	None
Subjects taught on the DVD:	Physical education; core, GCSE and 'A' level
Year group taught on the VITAL DVD:	Year 8

Les Taggart – Key Elements

These are my initial ideas on some of the characteristics that make Les an effective teacher:

1 warmth of personality

2 clarity of instructions

3 a positive use of questions and answers

4 sincere praise

5 the use of kinaesthetic instructions

6 a sense of humour

7 use of the unexpected

8 entertainment as a learning tool

9 congruence of messages

10 genuine enthusiasm

11 subject expertise

12 clear lesson structure

13 the use of the names of pupils

14 reliability and integrity.

Key Element 1 – Warmth of personality

One of the things which I believe is instantly noticeable about Les is the warmth of his personality. It may be true to say that this is not something that is easy to mirror, but it is an undeniable strength in a teacher's toolkit. To some extent the warmth a teacher demonstrates can develop and flourish once he is confident in what he is doing. There is a clear symbiotic relationship between a teacher's warmth and his confidence: they nourish one another. However, like the TV newsreader who has to remain apparently calm and cool when the video footage fails to appear or the autocue she is reading from disappears, so a teacher must display calm in all circumstances in the classroom. This initial act of remaining calm will develop into something that becomes more natural when the teacher experiences the effectiveness of it. Calm control will become the norm, and warmth of personality will develop as a result. Les's relationship with his pupils has been built up over a number of years. Warmth within the classroom will bring respect from the pupils through the confidence they gain from the teacher. Pupil confidence will also develop from the following key element.

Q11.   **Warmth**. What techniques can you think of that would bring even greater warmth to your classroom persona?

Effective Teachers in Secondary Schools

Key Element 2 – Clarity of instructions

Les issues instructions with clarity and gives his pupils confidence in the work they are doing with him. He adopts a central position in the gym and is always in full control of the group and the activity. His hand gestures are both reassuring and natural – but it is possible for anyone to copy these so that they become natural in appearance and, over a period of time, a 'habit'. He displays great confidence in his own ability and his right to be the teacher, but without any hint of an aggressive stance.

Following an activity, Les demonstrated a simple but very effective technique for getting the pupils to come to a standstill: the class is asked to do a jump-stop when he blows the whistle. This brings them immediately to a standstill ready for the next instruction. Teachers in classrooms (and also games teachers) sometimes find it hard to get pupils to stop one activity and receive the instructions for another. This can be a cause of great stress and it is important, no matter what technique is used, that pupils become familiar with the signal a teacher uses to get back their attention.

Q12. **Clarity**. What signals do you use with your classes? (These can sometimes be very subtle.)

Key Element 3 – Positive use of questions and answers

Les uses questions and answers as a key element of the lesson. There are some people who claim that the use of direct questions by a teacher can be counterproductive, with only a few pupils actively participating in the process and others largely dissociated from the activity. I understand that this can indeed be the case when classes are either reluctant to answer questions for fear of being ridiculed by their peers, or when they are simply not interested and motivated by the prospect of answering questions. It clearly works in this situation for Les, however, and is a critical part of the way he conducts the lesson.

Q13. **Questioning**. What questioning techniques do you use to elicit the maximum response from all students?

Key Element 4 – Sincere praise

A key element in the repertoire of any successful teacher is the use of praise. There is a rule of thumb that any negative comment directed at a pupil should be balanced by at least five positives. Les repeatedly gives positive feedback and encouragement. This succeeds as well as it does because it is *sincerely* given. The *intention* of a teacher is very important. In other words, if a positive comment is given, but does not match with what the class perceives as the real feelings of the teacher, then there is a lack of congruity. This will result in the class feeling uneasy with the mixed messages they receive.

Q14. **Positives**. Do you keep a mental record of how many positives to negatives you use in the classroom?

Key Element 5 – Use of kinaesthetic instructions

Les employs a very kinesthetic style in the way he carries out his lesson. He instructs the class by physically demonstrating the actions himself. Clearly, being a games teacher naturally involves more opportunities for the use of the kinesthetic, but I would suggest that all teachers could learn from watching games teachers and incorporating their techniques into classroom-based activities.

Q15. See Q9.

Key Element 6 – A sense of humour

We all want to have a good time. Adolescents may at times give a different impression and their idea of a good time does not always match that of a teacher – or indeed their parents. But deep down we all want to be happy and content. The use of humour allows the class to see that the teacher is relaxed and comfortable with them – that he is indeed happy to be with them. Les demonstrates understated humour on a number of occasions and this undoubtedly adds to the general impression of control he has.

Q16. See Q6.

Key Element 7 – Use of the unexpected

This can be a useful way of constantly re-engaging pupils' attention and keeping them wondering what will happen next. When you watch Les you will see that he subtly uses the unexpected to move the lesson along and maintain pupils' attention.

Q17. **The unexpected**. Do you bring an element of surprise into your teaching script?

Key Element 8 – Entertainment as a learning tool

A good teacher will entertain a class. Again, this can be done in a variety of ways but it will significantly reduce the probability of a class becoming bored and as a result disruptive. A good teacher is a good performer – a good actor. The need for a teacher to be an actor was mentioned earlier and a number of the teachers in the VITAL project independently referred to acting skills as an important ingredient in the effectiveness of a teacher. Les naturally gives a good performance which constantly engages pupils' attention.

Q18. **Entertainment**. Do you constantly try to bring new lines into your teaching script?

Key Element 9 – Congruence of messages

It is important that the different messages the pupils get from the teacher are matched, or congruent. If a teacher says one thing in words (e.g. 'Well done, John') but her tone of voice doesn't express that she is pleased with the work, then the pupil will get mixed messages and feel confused. What is said, how it is said, body language and facial expression should all match for the pupil to feel secure and confident. Les demonstrates congruence with each of these aspects.

Q19. See Q10.

Key Element 10 – Genuine enthusiasm

Les displays a genuine enthusiasm for the work he is doing with his pupils. A class will very rapidly pick up the message that the teacher is not particularly interested in the work they are doing. It is then little wonder if they respond by showing little enthusiasm themselves.

Q20. **Enthusiasm**. What strategies do you employ to maintain your enthusiasm for teaching?

Key Element 11 – Subject expertise

Les demonstrates a good level of competence in the topic he is teaching. Clearly, a level of teacher expertise in the subject taught is useful. Some may say it is essential, and certainly in a number of subjects it is important that the correct facts are given. It is no good a teacher teaching about the Battle of Hastings in 1066 but getting the outcome of the battle wrong. In a similar way it is no good a physics teacher going through the Theory of Special Relativity with a sixth form class without understanding the fundamental concepts herself. Due to timetabling commitments and constraints most teachers will have experienced teaching at times subjects which they are not so familiar with. As a result they will also have experienced the discomfort brought by pupils who ask questions and reveal the teacher's limited knowledge and understanding of the subject. With the inevitable changes brought about by information technology in the structure and content of lessons, teachers will at times have to adapt even more to not always knowing answers to the questions the class may ask. At times they will be on a journey of discovery with the class, which for some will be exciting and for others will present a new, threatening environment. Then the examples of effective teaching we are looking at in VITAL will be even more important.

Q21. **Subject expertise**. If a student asks you a question to which you do not know the answer (although you may think that you should), how do you deal with this? It is important to think through how you might react before it happens.

Key Element 12 – Clear lesson structure

Les's lesson has a very clear progression throughout. There is no doubt that the pupils will have gained new knowledge and expertise by the end of the lesson, and in his interview on the video you will hear Les emphasizing the importance of all pupils achieving something. A teacher should always have clear aims and objectives for every lesson he teaches. Then he can set a series of challenges which all the pupils in the class can benefit from.

Q22. **Structure**. Do you ensure that the aims and objectives of your lessons are as clear to the student, as they are to you?

Key Element 13 – Using pupils' names

Les uses the names of pupils when he addresses them in the lesson. Getting to know the class is very important. The use of a person's name is a very powerful tool, and pupils will respond much better when the teacher uses their names and thus demonstrates an interest in them.

Q23. **Names**. Do you find the names of the students you teach easy to remember? If not, have you thought about ways of improving your recall?

Key Element 14 – Reliability and integrity

This is mentioned in the DfEE document *National Standards for Headteachers*, which says that this attribute is possessed and displayed by all successful and effective teachers. Being reliable and a person of integrity perhaps sums up the general feeling one experiences when watching Les in action.

Q24. **Integrity**. How do you establish integrity with the students you teach? Write your answer down and refer to it regularly.

Les Taggart – direct links with the Hay McBer Report Teaching skills

The following describes the links I have made between Les' teaching and the Hay McBer Report. As for all the teachers I have chosen one Teaching Skill and three Professional Characteristics.

Teaching Skill

The Teaching Skill from the Hay McBer Report that I have chosen to link Les with is:

   A High expectations

One of the key questions the Hay McBer Report asks about 'high expectations' is:

> ▸ *Does the teacher provide opportunities for students to take responsibility for their own learning?*

Les gives very clear instructions, but within a framework that allows pupils to learn from their own experience, sometimes failing but always supported by positive correction and encouragement. The quotation I have used at the beginning of this section on Les and taken from his interview shows how his views on this match those of the Hay McBer Report.

Professional Characteristics

The three Professional Characteristics from the Hay McBer Report that I have chosen to link with les are:

Cluster	Characteristics
A Professionalism	**II** Creating trust
B Planning and setting expectations	**II** Drive for improvement
D Leading	**II** Holding people accountable

A Professionalism – Creating trust

Under Professional Characteristics and within the cluster of **A** Professionalism, the Hay McBer Report emphasizes the importance of *creating trust*:

> *Being sincere and genuine creates an atmosphere of trust, and allows pupils to act naturally, express themselves honestly, and not be afraid of making mistakes – an essential starting point for learning. It also helps build rapport with pupils.*

Les is sincere and genuine in his approach with the pupils. He is never patronizing but he demands high standards whilst allowing pupils to make mistakes and encouraging them to learn by trying. Les creates trust through key elements such as:

- warmth of personality
- clarity of instruction
- sincere praise
- the use of pupils' names
- reliability and integrity.

C Planning and setting expectations – Drive for improvement

Under Professional Characteristics and within the cluster of **C** Planning and setting expectations, the Hay McBer Report emphasizes the importance of the *drive for improvement*:

> *This is about moving out of the comfort zone and providing challenge and excitement in the learning process.*

The pupils Les teaches are clearly challenged and are stimulated by the learning environment he provides for them. Les talks in his interview about wanting all pupils, from the least to the most able, to be challenged by his lessons while feeling that they have all achieved something. This is very important because it is essential that pupils should feel a sense of achievement and that they can succeed. Pupils who feel that the challenge is too great will simply turn off, and this is often the cause of dissatisfaction and resultant discipline problems in a classroom. Les's emphasis on a drive for improvement permeates all he does and is exemplified by key elements such as:

- a clear lesson structure.

D Leading – Holding people accountable

Under Professional Characteristics and within the cluster of **D** Leading, the Hay McBer Report emphasizes the importance of *holding people accountable*:

> *Stating expectations and defining boundaries are needed in order to focus learning and minimize distraction. Clarifying accountability builds a sense of community with shared norms of behaviour. Clear and predictable routines create safety and security.*

Safety and security are essential foundations for the lessons of any PE teacher – but this is true in all lessons. Without feeling safe and secure, pupils cannot learn. Les speaks with calm authority and there is little doubt that he expects high standards; and as a result this is what he and his pupils experience. Les creates a 'sense of community with shared norms of behaviour' through his interaction with the pupils. The following key elements are crucial in this:

- positive use of questions and answers

- a sense of humour

- congruence of message

- subject expertise.

Neil Pointon

I think I'm a bit of an actor, and I walk the plank each day.

Neil Pointon

Neil Pointon – VITAL Teacher Profile

Age when filmed:	52
School:	Roundhay School in Leeds
Number of pupils in the school:	Approximately 1,400
Age range:	11 to 18
Age range Neil teaches:	11 to 18
Date he joined this school:	1988
Total years of teaching:	12
Previous schools:	None
Subjects taught on the DVD:	Chemistry Science Maths
Year group taught on the VITAL DVD:	Year 10

Neil Pointon – Key Elements

These are my initial ideas on some of the characteristics that make Neil an effective teacher:

1 giving a number of degrees of freedom

2 closeness to the pupils

3 pupil respect

4 gentle and unthreatening guidance

5 warmth and humour

6 calling out answers

7 a calm manner

8 knowing the pupils

9 adaptability to changing circumstances and new ideas.

Key Element 1 – Giving a number of degrees of freedom

The level of freedom allowed in a lesson is very important to the overall impact the lesson has on the pupils. Neil shows great confidence in giving a lot of responsibility and ownership for learning to the pupils. This allows the pupils to discover for themselves by a process of trial and error.

Q25. **Freedom**. How do you bring personal exploration and discovery into your lessons?

Key Element 2 – Closeness to the pupils

Neil's style involves him working closely on a one-to-one basis with pupils, answering their individual questions. His comments on the video about how he uses some of the skills he has learned from acting in his interactions with pupils are interesting and may be tried by other teachers.

Q26. **Closeness**. Do you ensure that in lessons you visit all parts of the classroom to be physically close to students? Are there any 'no-go' areas in your classroom? If so, how will you deal with this?

Key Element 3 – Gaining the respect of pupils

Neil's pupils clearly like him. They respect his authority but they are confident enough to put forward their own views. Neil works with them through a negotiating style. 'We are working together' is implicit in all he does with the class. This requires a level of maturity from the pupils, but it can develop when they are given more ownership for their individual learning.

Q27. **Respect**. How do you set out to gain respect from students? It is worth reminding yourself of the methods you use on a regular basis.

Key Element 4 – Gentle and unthreatening guidance

Neil employs a subtle style of mirroring the pupils to create empathy. He alludes to this in his interview and has gained these skills through experience and learning the skills of the actor. Through this approach he gives his pupils guidance without ever being dictatorial.

Q28. **Mirroring**. What mirroring techniques do you use in the classroom?

Key Element 5 – Warmth and humour

Neil demonstrates in all that he does that he likes working with his pupils. There is a warmth and a sincerity which they find comforting. Coupled with this is an underlying humour which breaks down any barriers that might otherwise exist.

Q29. See Q11.

Key Element 6 – Calling out answers

Neil allows the pupils to call out answers when they are around him at the end of the lesson. They do this with confidence and it eliminates the slower process of question/hand-up/selection of pupil/response from pupil/feedback on response from the teacher. It lets pupils feel they can answer questions more freely (they like to instantly call out a response) but it never gets out of control. This works well here and it is something to consider. A teacher could give the class a signal at times that they can just instantly give responses, whereas at other times putting up their hands first may be thought to be more appropriate. Variation and experimentation with these techniques is the important thing.

Q30. **Answers**. How do you vary the ways in which students are able to give responses or answers to questions?

Key Element 7 – A calm manner

Neil has a calm manner throughout the lesson. This gives pupils a feeling of being in a safe, structured and secure environment where learning can therefore flourish.

Q31. **Calm**. How do you establish a calm atmosphere in your classroom?

Key Element 8 – Knowing the pupils

Neil demonstrates that he knows his pupils very well. He says that this is something that he feels is crucial in his teaching. He knows who they are and what they are about and this assists the smooth running of his lessons. He uses their names and communicates with them on an intimate but, at the same time, controlled basis.

Q32. **Knowing the pupils**. How do you actively seek ways to find out what makes students tick?

Key Element 9 – Adaptability to changing circumstances and new ideas

This is mentioned in the DfEE document *National Standards for Headteachers*, which says that this attribute is possessed and displayed by all successful and effective teachers. Neil demonstrates that he is willing to listen to the pupils' views and not be simply led by his own initial idea. Within the framework of a well-structured lesson, he therefore allows scope for growth, adaptability and development.

Q33. **Adaptability**. Change in education is inevitable. Do you have a mindset that embraces this inevitability?

Neil Pointon – direct links with the Hay McBer Report

The following describes the links I have made between Neil's teaching and the Hay McBer Report. As for all the teachers, I have chosen one Teaching Skill and three Professional Characteristics.

Teaching Skill

The Teaching Skill from the Hay McBer Report that I have chosen to link Neil with is:

B Planning

Two of the key questions the Hay McBer Report asks about 'methods and strategies' are:

> ▶ *Does the teacher have the necessary materials and resources ready for the lesson?*
>
> ▶ *Does the teacher review what the pupils have learned at the end of the lesson?*

Neil's lesson has many elements to it in terms of what avenue of investigation the pupils may choose to go down. This has clearly got to happen within the framework of a well-structured lesson in which there is a variety of equipment that the pupils can choose from. The materials and resources need to be available so that the lesson can flow. Flow in a lesson is very important, with different elements of the lesson knitting seamlessly together to make a coherent whole. Neil also makes a point of getting the pupils around him at the end of the lesson to review the findings in the lesson, the possible ways methods could be improved on and the successes the class has experienced.

Professional Characteristics

The three Professional Characteristics from the Hay McBer Report that I have chosen to link with Neil are:

Cluster	Characteristics
A Professionalism **B** Thinking **D** Planning and setting expectations	**II** Respect for others **II** Conceptual thinking **II** Information seeking

A Professionalism – Respect for others

Under Professional Characteristics and within the cluster of **A** Professionalism, the Hay McBer Report emphasizes the importance of *respect for others:*

> *Listening to others and valuing their contribution is fundamental to the empathy and exchange that is at the heart of education and learning.*

This is an intrinsic part of Neil's negotiating style. He listens to what his pupils say and in some ways learns from them, as well as helping them. The Hay McBer Report mentions how a teacher who demonstrates respect for others helps pupils to become good citizens. This allows pupils to experiment, putting forward suggestions with confidence, and motivates them to succeed – perhaps far more than they ever believed possible. An open atmosphere of sharing views also helps pupils to develop a sense of community in the class and in the school. The Hay McBer Report also says:

> *Respect for others underpins everything the effective teacher does, and is expressed in a constant concern that everyone should treat pupils and all members of the school community with respect.*

The key elements which exemplify the way in which Neil shows respect for others include:

▸ giving a number of degrees of freedom

▸ pupil respect

▸ gentle and unthreatening guidance

▸ calling out answers

B Thinking – Conceptual thinking

Under Professional Characteristics and within the cluster of **B** Thinking, the Hay McBer Report emphasizes the importance of the drive for *conceptual thinking*:

> *They therefore move easily between the big picture and the detail.*

Encouraging pupils to endeavour to grasp concepts is often extremely difficult because it involves high-level thinking, and therefore can cause 'pain'. Grasping concepts can, however, be extremely fulfilling for both the pupils and the teacher. It requires the freedom for the individual to fail before succeeding, and this can only happen in a classroom environment which allows and values the views of individuals. Neil demonstrates how he often helps pupils to understand something very complex by gently guiding them and coaxing answers from them without directly and instantly giving them the answer. This will allow them to move from the detail to the big picture.

Key elements which illustrate Neil's ability with pupils in this respect include:

▸ giving a number of degrees of freedom

▸ gentle and unthreatening guidance

▸ adaptability to new ideas and changing circumstances.

C Planning and setting expectations – Information seeking

Under 'professional characteristics' and within the cluster of **C** Planning and setting **expectations**, the Hay McBer Report emphasizes the importance of *information seeking*:

> ▸ ... *having a deeper understanding of pupils, their background, who they are. And their prior learning and attainment helps teachers know what will interest and motivate them, so they can adapt their own approach. As a result, pupils are likely to feel recognized and valued as individuals.*
>
> ▸ *Finding appropriate resources and the best practice of others enhances teaching and learning, keeps approaches and programmes of work fresh, and avoids reinventing the wheel, ensuring effort is not wasted. Seeking out relevant inspection and research evidence can help improve planning and teaching.*

The first statement defines an element that is absolutely crucial for an effective teacher. The more we can get to know our pupils, the more we will understand their needs and what influences them. We will also get to appreciate their particular preferred method of learning and therefore provide lessons which accommodate this. Neil talks in the interview about the importance of getting to know pupils, and in his interactions with them that we see on the DVD it is evident that he has a good grasp of each one as an individual.

The second statement is really what VITAL is all about. We must all be students or lifelong learners wishing to find new and better ways of doing what we do – however effective we may already be. There is a vast amount of good practice which we can share and continually learn from each other as teachers. Neil mentions in his interview how he is always learning. Key elements which support Neil in this respect are:

▸ closeness to the pupils

▸ knowing the pupils.

Phil Hardy

What I have learned is that it is much more effective to use positive measures and rewards rather than negative measures.

Phil Hardy

Phil Hardy – VITAL Teacher Profile

Age when filmed:	44
School:	Crawshaw School
Number of pupils in the school:	Approximately 1,150
Age range:	11 to 18
Age range Phil teaches:	11 to 18
Date he joined this school:	1984
Total years of teaching:	20
Previous schools:	Garforth Comprehensive
Subjects taught on the DVD:	History (Also Head of History and ITT Coordinator)
Year group taught on the VITAL DVD:	Year 9

Phil Hardy – Key Elements

These are my initial ideas on some of the characteristics that make Phil an effective teacher:

1 involvement with the pupils

2 using pupils' names

3 showing respect for pupils

4 encouraging thinking

5 use of praise

6 having a sense of humour

7 enthusiasm for teaching

8 gaining the respect of pupils

9 commitment.

Key Element 1 – Involvement with the pupils

Phil has a very close physical presence with the class. He achieves this when he is standing up and talking to the class by constantly moving around. Then, when the pupils are involved in group-work, he brings a warm and authoritative presence to all groups in the room. A teacher who always stands at the front of the class or, worse still, behind a desk will appear to be afraid to enter into the province of the pupils – to be hiding behind a barricade. The classroom should be open in all areas with no 'no-go' areas for anyone – and certainly not the teacher.

Q34. **Connecting**. How do your ensure that you relate to pupils?

Key Element 2 – Using pupils' names

I have referred to this with other teachers: the use of the pupils' names is such a simple but powerful tool. The truth of this is perhaps only really apparent when observing a teacher who does not use pupils' names.

It is very interesting to listen to politicians being interviewed on television or radio. They often use the name of the person they are interviewing and this immediately brings a sense of warmth and familiarity which helps the flow of the general discussion they are having. I think Tony Blair was a master at this, and deliberately used this tool whenever he could, whether in an interview or talking to a member of the public. It may be argued that this is deliberate manipulation and just one part of the so-called 'spin doctor' approach of the Labour Party, but the more relaxed and friendly feeling it engenders is hard to deny. Business people have also learned the value and power of using the Christian names of people they are talking to over the phone or face to face.

Our names are important to us – you only have to see the reaction of people when their names are spelled incorrectly or they are called by the wrong name, to understand this. Teachers who use the names of pupils will therefore have a real advantage in their interactions, whether in the classroom or around the school. The last thing a pupil wants when doing something they shouldn't be doing around the school is for a teacher to call out their name and ask them to come over. They feel far more secure and anonymous when the teacher has to resort to 'You, come over here', and indeed this can often be the trigger for the beginning of a long and potentially conflict-driven interaction between the teacher and pupil.

Q35.   See Q23.

Key Element 3 – Showing respect for pupils

Phil's whole manner shows respect for his pupils. He refers to this as well in his interview:

When pupils give their responses and suggestions, Phil is constantly feeding back praise. Showing respect for pupils will help to generate respect the other way. However difficult it

I always respect pupils – every pupil I teach will always eventually be aware, through explicit or implicit means, that I respect them.

may be, and as teachers we have all found situations where pupils have tested our altruistic feelings, we must dissociate the action of a pupil from the person themselves. In doing this we can show respect for the individual while being free to criticize their actions. Comments such as 'You are a cheeky boy' will therefore just reinforce the behaviour which is being criticized. The pupil has been told he is cheeky, so he might as well continue to be cheeky in the future, and even in the present interaction with the teacher. Unless the teacher is lucky, a conflict spiral is therefore almost certain to develop. On the other hand, saying, 'The way you spoke just now is not appropriate, Susan. It's not what I expect from you' is referring to an action – which the pupil can more readily accept, as it is not criticizing them as a person.

Q36.   **Respect for pupils**. Among the ways that you demonstrate respect for pupils, are you aware of referring to behaviour and not the person themselves (unless the reference is to something positive)?

Key Element 4 – Encouraging thinking

A key part of the lesson shown here involves Phil eliciting the views of the class. This requires the class to think. Phil could have simply given the class the information, but getting them to think and come up with their own views is far more powerful as a teaching and learning tool. Thinking skills are now becoming a central part of the curriculum in many schools, with a growing understanding of the different ways that pupils can access information to enable them to comprehend work more effectively. Teachers often feel under pressure to get through the syllabus, and an apparently simple way of achieving this is to didactically teach a class. Most teachers now realize, however, that this is not necessarily the best way to get pupils either to understand or to recall work.

Q37.   **Thinking**. Do you provide moments for deep thinking in your lessons? This can be very powerful.

Key Element 5 – The use of praise

Phil gives this almost continuously – not in a casual way, but with sincerity and thought. His pupils, therefore, feel that they have earned their praise 'reward'.

Q38.   See Q14.

Key Element 6 – Having a sense of humour

Another key tool in Phil's armoury is his sense of humour. I have referred to this with other teachers in VITAL and it really is an important part of a teacher's repertoire. Phil confirms this in his interview, and there is a central thread of humour throughout his entire lesson.

Q39. See **Q6**.

Key Element 7 – Enthusiasm for teaching

Like all effective teachers, Phil displays a real enthusiasm for teaching and a deep knowledge of his subject. He communicates this in a very down-to-earth-manner with pupils, using simple methods to stimulate them further. This may involve him simply saying things like 'That's three–nil, isn't it', when pupils volunteer their opinions. In doing this he is immediately sharing the lesson and the enthusiasm he has with the pupils.

Q40. **Enthusiasm**. How do you convey the passion you have for what you are teaching?

Key Element 8 – Gaining the respect of pupils

The pupils obviously respect Phil. The main reason for this, I believe, is that they know that he cares about them and respects them. This is linked with all the other key elements already mentioned.

Q41. See **Q27**.

Key Element 9 – Commitment

This is mentioned in the DfEE document *National Standards for Headteachers*, which says that this attribute is possessed and displayed by all successful and effective teachers. Pupils know when the teacher is working for them and they will respond positively to this. Phil is clearly committed to developing as a teacher. He is also clearly committed to doing the very best for all the pupils he teaches.

Q42. **Commitment**. How do you demonstrate to students that you are committed to helping them?

Phil Hardy – direct links with the Hay McBer Report

The following describes the links I have made between Phil's teaching and the Hay McBer Report. As for all the teachers, I have chosen one Teaching Skill and three Professional Characteristics.

Teaching Skill

The Teaching Skill from the Hay McBer Report that I have chosen to link Phil with is:

  D Pupil management / discipline

Two of the key questions the Hay McBer Report asks about 'Pupil management/discipline' are:

> ▶ *Does the teacher treat praise good achievement and effort?*
>
> ▶ *Does the teacher treat different children fairly?*

It is very clear from watching Phil that he does both of these things, as a natural and integral part of his lesson.

The Hay McBer Report says that highly effective teachers are able to 'create an environment in which all pupils can learn by employing direct means of pupil management to ensure that disruption to pupil learning is minimized and pupils feel safe and secure'. The 'lighthouse effect' in teaching is important, such that teachers are aware of everything that is going on around them in the classroom and that in addition they 'catch them being good' so that appropriate pupil behaviour is recognized and reinforced with praise.

Professional Characteristics

The three Professional Characteristics from the Hay McBer Report that I have chosen to link with Phil are:

Cluster	Characteristics
A Professionalism	**II** Challenge and support
D Leading	**II** Flexibility
E Relating to others	**II** Teamworking

A Professionalism – Challenge and support

Under 'professional characteristics' and within the cluster of **A** Professionalism, the Hay McBer Report emphasizes the importance of *challenge and support:*

The report goes on to say:

> *Expressing positive expectations of pupils – that they can and will learn and be successful – is one of the most powerful ways to influence pupils and raise achievement. It is one of the distinctive behaviours of high performing teachers who radiate confidence in their pupils and their potential, and never give up on them.*

Phil expects a lot of the pupils he teaches, and this gives them confidence to do well.

> *Effective teachers also provide **challenge and support** – a 'tough caring' where they not only cater for pupils' needs for physical and psychological safety but, crucially, repeatedly express positive expectations and build pupils' self-esteem and belief that they can succeed, as learners and in life.*

When he refers to 'not expecting that kind of answer from a Year 9 pupil ... that is GCSE standard', he boosts not only the confidence of the pupil he is referring to but also the class as a whole. He says this genuinely and with authority based on experience. It is well understood that pupils will only learn well when they are not anxious but rather comfortable and confident. Phil provides the comfort and confidence they need to grow as individuals. Giving pupils the feeling that they can succeed raises their self confidence and self-esteem.

Ways in which Phil challenges and supports pupils include the key elements:

- showing respect for pupils

- encouraging thinking

- the use of praise.

D Leading – Flexibility

Under 'professional characteristics' and within the cluster of **D** Leading, the Hay McBer Report emphasizes the importance of *flexibility*:

It is crucial that an effective teacher should be prepared to adapt to changing situations

Spontaneity generates vitality, helps to make it enjoyable, and may help growth of creative and imaginative approaches to problem-solving.

and change tactics when appropriate. What an individual pupil brings into the classroom can often stimulate a learning experience which an effective teacher will seize on. An effective teacher will react to pupil responses and take advantage of unexpected events.

Key elements which illustrate Phil's flexibility include:

- showing respect for pupils

- encouraging thinking.

E Relating to others – Teamworking

Under 'professional characteristics' and within the cluster of **E** Relating to others, the Hay McBer Report emphasizes the importance of *teamworking*:

One of the roles Phil has in his school is that of being an ITT Coordinator. He refers in

Teamwork between school colleagues, including support staff and others in the school community, is necessary to ensure an integrated and coherent approach that makes sense to pupils and facilitates their learning.

the interview to learning as much from the skills ITT students bring into the school as the students learn during their teaching experience. Teaching is a lifelong learning experience, and a great way of learning in a school is to operate as a team and benefit from the knowledge and experience of each individual. This encourages shared goals and greater effectiveness.

Mark Birch

 There should never be a period when they are doing a task and they haven't been given a concrete time in which to perform it.

Mark Birch

Mark Birch – VITAL Teacher Profile

Age when filmed:	30
School:	Benton Park School in Leeds
Number of pupils in the school:	Approximately 1,400
Age range:	11 to 18
Age range Mark teaches:	11 to 18
Date he joined this school:	2000
Total years of teaching:	6
Previous schools:	Collenswood Comprehensive in Stevenage Garforth Community School in Leeds
Subjects taught on the DVD:	English
Year group taught on the VITAL DVD:	Year 9

Mark Birch – Key Elements

These are my initial thoughts concerning the characteristics that make Mark an effective teacher.

1 the skills of an orator

2 relaxed body language

3 giving precise and specific instructions / references

4 good subject knowledge/expertise

5 praise / use of pupils' names

6 a sense of humour

7 making reference to youth culture

8 making reference to your own experience

9 create visual images

10 giving a time allowance for tasks

11 obvious enthusiasm and love of your subject

12 a clear structure and overall plan

13 intellectual ability.

Mark's style shown in the DVD evidence is very individual and some may argue that it would be hard to mimic unless a storytelling approach is part of your repertoire. As I have indicated previously, however, I believe that it is possible to try out many different kinds of approach, and learn from everyone observed. The key is to mirror another teacher's style until it becomes part of your nature or a 'habit'.

Key Element 1 – The skills of an orator

One of Mark's tools, which he uses very successfully here, is that of an orator. There can be a danger in teaching that too much talking is done by the teacher – John Freeman, as an adviser in Leeds over a number of years, says that this is perhaps his greatest general criticism of teachers. The voice, however, is clearly one of the chief ways of communicating, and just as the quality of our life is the quality of our communication, so the quality of our teaching depends significantly on our ability to verbally communicate with clarity. Mark not only speaks with clarity but is also a good storyteller. The skills of an orator have an important role in engaging the imagination of pupils in teaching. Any teacher who has experienced having the class in the palm of their hand as they relate some experience or explain a certain concept will know the power of the delivery of words.

Q43. **Storytelling**. Do you practise the stories you tell students to enhance your lessons?

Key Element 2 – A relaxed body language

Mark displays great confidence through his body language. He looks totally comfortable with his place in the classroom as the teacher, and this gives the pupils confidence. This, and the skills of an orator, are clearly essential ingredients in the toolkit of an actor. Just as actors are trained and tutored in these skills, so I believe there is a place for them in education for teachers. A later VITAL project will concentrate wholly on the way in which acting skills can be learned and employed by teachers.

Q44. See **Q2**.

Key Element 3 – Giving precise and specific instructions/references

Mark gives the class an early indication of why the work they are doing is important. He refers directly to their SATS, and specifically mentions 'Section C of Paper 1', for example. The pupils know, therefore, that success in what they are about to do will pay dividends in something which is important to them. This class is an able group and Mark's pitch of the lesson suits their ability. All classes, however, should be engaged in work by understanding the importance of what they are doing. None of us likes to do work in which we have no investment. Pupils are, of course, no different in this respect. (The same idea of investment applies to their behaviour. Pupils only misbehave when the attention they receive for doing so pays more dividends than the dividend they receive for their investment in good behaviour.)

Q45. **Instructions**. Are you aware of how clearly you give instructions? Would you be able to get feedback about this from the students themselves?

Key Element 4 – Good subject knowledge/expertise

Mark is clearly very comfortable with his subject knowledge. Pupils will sense this and it will of course give them confidence. A teacher who is an expert in his subject will tend to be more flexible and receptive to the demands of individuals and different classes.

Q46. See **Q21**.

Key Element 5 – Praise/use of pupils' names

Like Les, Mark gives out a lot of *praise*. All effective teachers do this. Because they receive praise, pupils are also given the confidence necessary to contribute their own views – and again, positive aspects of their contributions can be highlighted and rewarded with praise. When talking to his pupils, Mark uses their names. Our names are important to all of us as human beings. Like all of us, pupils will respond more positively to being referred to by their names rather than impersonal pointing or 'you'.

Q47. See **Q14** and **Q23**.

Key Element 6 – A sense of humour

Having a sense of humour doesn't imply that a teacher should be telling jokes all the time – though a well-thought-out joke in the context of a lesson can be a very powerful motivator. Mark, however, employs humour in a number of subtle ways. He talks about 'bed to bed' stories, uses an unusual voice and refers to things as being 'so dull'. All of this helps the pupils to relate to him as an individual. These things seem so simple, but like all good practice in classroom management they are vital ingredients.

Q48. See **Q6.**

Key Element 7 – Making reference to youth culture

This is another way of relating to pupils. Mark uses references to Robbie Williams and his video *Rock DJ*, which the pupils will immediately associate with. Pupils will immediately think, 'Oh, he knows about this', and see the teacher more as an individual! Mark also relates to both boys and girls through the use of humorous stereotypical stories. (Teachers must always be wary of offending pupils, or indeed anyone else, by what they say. But a bit of common sense and knowing your audience allows you to feel freedom to talk in a professional and open manner to a class.)

Q49. **Youth culture**. Do you make an active attempt to raise your awareness of the accepted culture of young people?

Key Element 8 – Making reference to your own experience

Mark refers to incidents and experiences from his own life. He makes reference to 'my mate Dave's sister' and the urban myth. The effect this has is, again, that the class will be able to relate to him more as an individual.

Q50. **Personal experience**. How do you ensure you relate to students through your own personal experience?

Key Element 9 – Create visual images

This links with earlier comments about Mark using his skills as an orator in the lessons. Mark uses his body and movement to bring life to the story he is telling. Small movements and uses of the body can bring a visual aspect to parts of a lesson which otherwise may be predominantly an auditory experience.

Q51. **Visual images**. Do you use words and body language as well as pictures to create vivid images?

Key Element 10 – Giving a time allowance for tasks

Mark mentions in his interview that he gives pupils a specific time to complete tasks. This is demonstrated in the classroom evidence on video when he gives the class three minutes to complete a task. The advantage of giving time allowances is that:

▶ pupils have a target for completing the work

▶ pupils don't have the time to be diverted into idle conversation

▶ pupils learn to work to specific deadlines.

Q52. **Time allocation**. Do you provide clear guidelines for the amount of time that students have to complete a task?

Effective Teachers in Secondary Schools

Key Element 11 – Obvious enthusiasm and love of your subject

Some people may have a tremendous knowledge of their subject but fail to enthral their pupils because they themselves seem to lack enthusiasm. Mark brings a fresh enthusiasm to his teaching, which will naturally inspire the pupils he teaches.

Q53. See **Q40**.

Key Element 12 – A clear structure and overall plan

In the lesson shown on the DVD there is a very clear start, middle and end. There is also no doubt that the pupils will have learned some valuable skills concerning essay construction by the time they leave the lesson – I certainly did by watching Mark!

Q54. See **Q22**.

Key Element 13 – Intellectual ability

This is mentioned in the DfEE document *National Standards for Headteachers*, which says that intellectual ability is possessed and displayed by all successful and effective teachers. I believe that this does not just mean a simple and narrow measure of a teacher's IQ. Rather, I believe it is a conscious awareness of all the multiple intelligences which teachers can draw on in themselves and also utilize with the pupils to produce a rich learning experience. Intelligence in the teacher therefore includes an understanding of preferred learning styles together with an appreciation of the emotional intelligence of individuals. (A good book for teachers to read concerning this is *Emotional Intelligence* by Daniel Goleman.)

Q55. **Emotional intelligence**. Are you aware of integrating aspects of emotional intelligence into your lessons?

Mark Birch – direct links with the Hay McBer Report

The following describes the links I have made between Mark's teaching and the Hay McBer Report. As for all the teachers, I have chosen one Teaching Skill and three Professional Characteristics.

Teaching Skill

The Teaching Skill from the Hay McBer Report that I have chosen to link Mark with is:

  E   Time and resource management

One of the key questions the Hay McBer Report asks about time and resource management is:

This clearly relates to the key element of a clear structure and overall plan.

> ▶ *Does the teacher structure the lesson to use the time available well?*

It is evident from the DVD that Mark manages the class by having a clear structure for the lesson. This enables him to be relaxed and confident. The Hay McBer Report talks about there being over 90 per cent of pupils on task with highly effective teachers. In Mark's lesson the pupils are eager to do the work and come up with their own individual contributions.

Professional Characteristics

The three professional characteristics identified in Mark from the Hay McBer Report are:

Cluster	Characteristics
B Thinking	**II** Analytical thinking
D Leading	**II** Flexibility
E Relating to others	**II** Impact and influence

B Thinking – Analytical thinking

Under Professional Characteristics and within the cluster of **B** Thinking, the Hay McBer Report emphasizes the importance of *analytical thinking*.

Effective lesson preparation takes into account the prior knowledge, understanding

> *Thoroughness in preparation, based on an accurate assessment of the stage pupils have reached – for the lesson, the term and the year – creates a framework for teaching and learning.*

and ability of pupils. Mark outlines at the beginning of the lesson the purpose of the work and how it fits into other work they have so far covered. The Hay McBer Report emphasizes the need for milestones to be specified 'so that pupils have a sense of progress and can measure their own achievements against learning objectives'. The report also suggests that by showing an analytical approach themselves, teachers will encourage pupils to adopt a logical approach and as a result question what and why they are doing things.

D Leading – Passion for learning

Under Professional Characteristics and within the cluster of **D** Leading, the Hay McBer Report emphasizes the importance of the *passion for learning*:

> *... the drive and an ability to support pupils in their learning, and to help them become confident and independent learners*

A teacher who demonstrates the importance of a passion for learning introduces pupils to independent learning skills which allows them to become lifelong learners. Such a teacher encourages pupils to work out answers for themselves. The following key elements are important in ensuring this:

- good subject knowledge/expertise
- obvious enthusiasm and love of your subject
- a clear structure and overall plan

E Relating to others – Impact and influence

Under Professional Characteristics and within the cluster of **E** Relating to others, the Hay McBer Report emphasizes the importance of *impact and influence*:

> *... does something that will make learning vivid or memorable. Consciously manages pace in a lesson to maximize learning outcomes.*

This links with the following key elements identified in Mark:

- making reference to youth culture
- making reference to your own experience
- create visual images
- good subject knowledge/expertise
- obvious enthusiasm and love of your subject.

Showing an enthusiasm for the subject encourages pupils to share that enthusiasm. The effective teacher will use a range of techniques to accomplish this, and as a result the pupils will want to be there and enjoy learning.

Section 6

Using the extended DVD highlights

The extended DVD highlights show approximately thirty minutes from each of the lessons of the five teachers.

To repeat what I have said earlier, the main aim of *Effective Teachers in Secondary Schools* is to give teachers a vehicle for looking at other teachers and as a result reflecting on their own classroom practice. If teachers benefit from this reflection then this in itself is enough and the principal reason why I embarked on the project. It is my strongly held view that we can all benefit from looking at the differing and similar practices we all adopt in the classroom. Observing teachers who adopt similar classroom management approaches to our own can be as rewarding as looking at teachers who employ different methods. It reassures us that our own classroom styles and management techniques are effectively employed by others, and in addition it can allow us to fine-tune these techniques. *Effective Teachers in Secondary Schools* has as its strong central basis the detailed work carried out by Hay McBer. By looking at and concentrating on developing the factors the Hay McBer Report highlighted, we can all be confident that we are moving in the right direction.

One way of approaching the extended highlights on the DVD is to use the observation form and guidance which I have provided in Appendices 1 and 2. The form and guidance are based on the Hay McBer categories of 'Teaching Skills', 'Professional Characteristics' and 'Classroom Climate'. (In the analysis of each teacher that I have provided earlier, I have concentrated on 'Teaching Skills' and 'Professional Characteristics' for the reasons I outlined.) Appendices 3, 4 and 5 then give further observation/self-analysis forms that further break down the teaching skills, professional characteristics and classroom climate into each of the elements. I recommend that these forms should not be used as a simple tick-box exercise. Rather, the aim is that they provide a way of giving meaningful feedback that can assist both ourselves and our colleagues to develop as reflective practitioners. So, for example, if your school (or your department) decides that 'Time and Resource Management' is something that classroom observations should concentrate on, then the observation form to use would be found in Appendix 3. (You would then select the fifth form in Appendix 3 with the title '5. Time and Resource Management'.) These forms can be used to observe each of the teachers in *Effective Teachers in Secondary Schools* and to write evidence for the particular 'Teaching Skills', 'Professional Characteristics' and 'Classroom Climate' you observe. You may then wish to refer back to the observations I have made about the particular teacher in this manual. For work in your own school these forms could then either be used as they stand or adapted by you or your school as a basis for carrying out 'Self-Evaluation' analysis, 'Monitoring and Evaluation' analysis or peer observation analysis of teaching styles in your school. You may then build up a catalogue of the kinds of expertise in particular teaching areas ('Teaching Skills', 'Professional Characteristics', or 'Classroom Climate') in your school so that all teachers will know where to go to see particular aspects of teacher effectiveness in the school. This sharing of good practice is to me crucial for the development of teaching and learning in schools.

You may on the other hand be about to apply to go through the 'Threshold' as a teacher, and I have attached an example of a blank Threshold Application form together with two examples of ways in which you may like to think about filling in your own form (Appendix 16). You may wish to use the filmed evidence of teachers in *Effective Teachers in Secondary Schools* to think about how you could most effectively move towards this important milestone in your teaching career.

Appendix 1: Linking Hay McBer Analysis with the Professional Standards for Teachers

Teaching Skills Observation Form

Note: References below refer to the Core Standards. For example C1 refers to Core Standard C1 in the Professional Standards for Teachers.

Date:	Teacher:
Lesson:	Observer:

Heading	Observations
1 High expectations Links with Core Standards C1 and C2	
2 Planning Links with Core Standards C3, C26 and C29	
3 Methods and strategies Links with Core Standards C29	
4 Pupil management/discipline Links with Core Standards C38 and C39	
5 Time and resource management	
6 Assessment Links with Core Standards C11, C12 and C13	
7 Homework Links with Core Standards C28 and C31	

Hay McBer – Professional Characteristics Observation Form

Date:	Teacher:
Lesson:	Observer:

Cluster	Tick characteristics to be observed	Observations
1 Professionalism	Challenge and support Confidence Creating trust Respect for others	
2 Thinking	Analytical thinking Conceptual thinking	
3 Planning and setting expectations	Drive for improvement Information seeking Initiative	
4 Leading	Flexibility Holding people accountable Managing pupils Passion for learning	
5 Relating to others	Impact and influence Teamworking Understanding others	

Hay McBer – Classroom Climate Observation Form

Date:	Teacher:
Lesson:	Observer:

Climate dimension	Observations
1 Clarity	
2 Order	
3 Standards	
4 Fairness	
5 Participation	
6 Support	
7 Safety	
8 Interest	
9 Environment	

Effective Teachers in Secondary Schools

Hay McBer Observation Guidance Criteria

Classroom Climate Guidance

Climate dimension	Guidance
1 Clarity	Clarity around the purpose of each lesson. How each lesson relates to the broader subject, as well as clarity regarding the aims and objectives of the school.
2 Order	Order within the classroom, where discipline, order and civilized behaviour are maintained.
3 Standards	A clear set of standards as to how pupils should behave and what each pupil should do and try to achieve, with a clear focus on higher rather than minimum standards.
4 Fairness	Fairness: the degree to which there is an absence of favouritism, and a consistent link between rewards in the classroom and actual performance.
5 Participation	Participation: the opportunity for pupils to participate actively in the class by discussion, questioning, giving out materials, and other similar activities.
6 Support	Support: feeling emotionally supported in the classroom, so that pupils are willing to try new things and learn from mistakes.
7 Safety	Safety: the degree to which the classroom is a safe place, where pupils are not at risk from emotional bullying, or other fear-rousing factors.
8 Interest	Interest: the feeling that the classroom is an interesting and exciting place to be, where pupils feel stimulated to learn.
9 Environment	Environment: the feeling that the classroom is a comfortable, well-organized, clean and attractive physical environment.

Appendix 3: Hay McBer Teaching Skills Forms – *for Self-analysis or Observation*

1. High expectations

Links with Core Standards C1 and C2

Effective teachers communicate high, clear and consistent expectations with an appropriate level of challenge to all pupils.

Key questions	Examples of how I do this
Does the teacher encourage high standards of effort, accuracy and presentation?	
Does the teacher use differentiation appropriately to challenge all pupils in the class?	
Does the teacher vary motivational strategies for different individuals?	
Does the teacher provide opportunities for students to take responsibility for their own learning?	
Does the teacher draw on pupil experiences or ideas relevant to the lesson?	

For free downloads of all these forms go to www.ecmconnections.co.uk

2. Planning

Links with Core Standards C3, C26 and C29

Effective teachers have a clear plan and objectives for each lesson. They communicate these clearly to pupils at the start of the session. They focus on pupils' learning outcomes. Learning activities have clear instructions.

Key questions	Examples of how I do this
Does the teacher communicate a clear plan and objectives for the lesson at the start of the lesson?	
Does the teacher have the necessary materials and resources ready for the class?	
Does the teacher link lesson objectives to the National Curriculum?	
Does the teacher review what pupils have learned at the end of the lesson?	

For free downloads of all these forms go to www.ecmconnections.co.uk

3. Methods and strategies

Links with Core Standard C29

Effective teachers use a variety of teaching strategies and techniques. They teach actively, interact a lot with pupils, and monitor their understanding. They keep pupils engaged and on task in class, small group and individual activities.

Key questions	Examples of how I do this
Does the teacher involve all pupils in the lesson?	
Does the teacher use a variety of activities/learning methods?	
Does the teacher apply teaching methods appropriate to the National Curriculum objectives?	
Does the teacher use a variety of questioning techniques to probe pupils' knowledge and understanding?	
Does the teacher encourage pupils to use a variety of problem-solving techniques?	
Does the teacher give clear instructions and explanations?	
Does practical activity have a clear purpose in improving pupils' understanding or achievement?	
Does the teacher listen and respond to pupils?	

For free downloads of all these forms go to www.ecmconnections.co.uk

Effective Teachers in Secondary Schools

4. Pupil management/discipline

Links with Core Standards C38 and C39

Effective teachers have a clear strategy for pupil management and communicate clear and effective boundaries for pupils' behaviour. Pupils feel safe and secure, and maximum time is focused on learning.

Key questions	Examples of how I do this
Does the teacher keep the pupils on task throughout the lesson?	
Does the teacher correct bad behaviour immediately?	
Does the teacher praise good achievement and effort?	
Does the teacher treat different children fairly?	
Does the teacher manage non-pupils (support teachers/ staff) well?	

For free downloads of all these forms go to www.ecmconnections.co.uk

5. Time and resource management

Effective teachers make full use of planned time, start promptly, maintain a brisk pace and finish with a succinct review of learning. They allocate their time fairly amongst pupils.

Key questions	Examples of how I do this
Does the teacher structure the lesson to use the time available well?	
Does the lesson last for the planned time?	
Are appropriate learning resources used to enhance pupils' opportunities?	
Does the teacher use an appropriate pace?	
Does the teacher allocate his/her time fairly amongst pupils?	

For free downloads of all these forms go to www.ecmconnections.co.uk

Effective Teachers in Secondary Schools

6. Assessment

Links with Core Standards C11, C12 and C13

Effective teachers make use of a range of assessment methods to monitor pupils' progress, their gaps in knowledge and areas of misunderstanding. They give feedback and encourage pupils to judge their own success and set themselves targets.

Key questions	Examples of how I do this
Does the teacher focus on understanding and meaning, factual memory, skills mastery and applications in real-life settings?	
Does the teacher use tests, competitions, etc. to assess understanding?	
Does the teacher recognize misconceptions and clear them up?	
Is there evidence of pupils' written work having been marked or otherwise assessed?	
Does the teacher encourage pupils to do better next time?	

For free downloads of all these forms go to www.ecmconnections.co.uk

7. Homework

Links with Core Standards C28 and C31

The regular setting of homework, in primary and secondary schools, is an important part of the assessment process. Effective teachers ensure that homework is integrated with class work, is tailored to individual needs and is marked regularly and constructively.

Key questions	Examples of how I do this
Is homework set either to consolidate or extend the coverage of the lesson?	
Is homework, which had been set previously, followed up in the lesson?	
Does the teacher explain what learning objectives pupils will gain from homework?	

For free downloads of all these forms go to www.ecmconnections.co.uk

Effective Teachers in Secondary Schools

Appendix 4: Hay McBer Professional Characteristics Forms – *for Self-analysis or Observation*

1. Professionalism

Characteristic	Self-analysis or Observation
Challenge and support A commitment to do everything possible for each pupil and enable all pupils to be successful.	
Confidence The belief in one's ability to be effective and to take on challenges.	
Creating trust Being consistent and fair. Keeping one's word.	
Respect for others The underlying belief that individuals matter and deserve respect.	

For free downloads of all these forms go to www.ecmconnections.co.uk

2. Thinking

Characteristic	Self-analysis or Observation
Analytical thinking The ability to think logically, break things down and recognize cause and effect.	
Conceptual thinking The ability to see patterns and links, even when there is a lot of detail.	

For free downloads of all these forms go to www.ecmconnections.co.uk

Effective Teachers in Secondary Schools

3. Planning and setting expectations

Characteristic	Self-analysis or Observation
Drive for improvement Relentless energy for setting and meeting challenging targets, for pupils and the school.	
Information seeking A drive to find out more and get to the heart of things; intellectual curiosity.	
Initiative The drive to act now to anticipate and pre-empt events.	

For free downloads of all these forms go to www.ecmconnections.co.uk

4. Leading

Characteristic	Self-analysis or Observation
Flexibility The ability and willingness to adapt to the needs of a situation and change tactics.	
Holding people accountable The drive and ability to set clear expectations and parameters and to hold others accountable for performance.	
Managing pupils The drive and the ability to provide clear direction to pupils, and to enthuse and motivate them.	
Passion for learning The drive and ability to support pupils in their learning, and how to help them become confident and independent learners.	

For free downloads of all these forms go to www.ecmconnections.co.uk

Effective Teachers in Secondary Schools

5. Relating to others

Characteristic	Self-analysis or Observation
Impact and influence The ability and the drive to produce positive outcomes by impressing and influencing others.	
Teamworking The ability to work with others to achieve shared goals.	
Understanding others The drive and ability to understand others, and why they behave as they do.	

For free downloads of all these forms go to www.ecmconnections.co.uk

Appendix 5: Hay McBer – Classroom Climate Forms – *for Self-analysis or Observation*

Key dimension	Self-analysis or Observation
1. Clarity Clarity around the purpose of each lesson. How each lesson relates to the broader subject, as well as clarity regarding the aims and objectives of the school.	
2. Order Order within the classroom, where discipline, order and civilized behaviour are maintained.	
3. Standards A clear set of standards as to how pupils should behave and what each pupil should do and try to achieve, with a clear focus on higher rather than minimum standards.	

For free downloads of all these forms go to www.ecmconnections.co.uk

Effective Teachers in Secondary Schools

Key dimension	Self-analysis or Observation
4. Fairness The degree to which there is an absence of favouritism, and a consistent link between rewards in the classroom and actual performance.	
5. Participation The opportunity for pupils to participate actively in the class by discussion, questioning, giving out materials, and other similar activities.	
6. Support Feeling emotionally supported in the classroom, so that pupils are willing to try new things and learn from mistakes.	

For free downloads of all these forms go to www.ecmconnections.co.uk

Key dimension	Self-analysis or Observation
7. Safety The degree to which the classroom is a safe place, where pupils are not at risk from emotional bullying, or other fear-rousing factors.	
8. Interest The feeling that the classroom is an interesting and exciting place to be, where pupils feel stimulated to learn.	
9. Environment The feeling that the classroom is a comfortable, well-organized, clean and attractive physical environment.	

For free downloads of all these forms go to www.ecmconnections.co.uk

Effective Teachers in Secondary Schools

Appendix 6: Professional Standards for Teachers – QTS Criteria

1. Professional attributes

Relationships with children and young people	
Q1	Have high expectations of children and young people including a commitment to ensuring that they can achieve their full educational potential and to establishing fair, respectful, trusting, supportive and constructive relationships with them.
Q2	Demonstrate the positive values, attitudes and behaviour they expect from children and young people.
Frameworks	
Q3	(a) Be aware of the professional duties of teachers and the statutory framework within which they work. (b) Be aware of the policies and practices of the workplace and share in collective responsibility for their implementation.
Communicating and working with others	
Q4	Communicate effectively with children, young people, colleagues, parents and carers.
Q5	Recognize and respect the contribution that colleagues, parents and carers can make to the development and well-being of children and young people, and to raising their levels of attainment.
Q6	Have a commitment to collaboration and co-operative working
Personal professional development	
Q7	(a) Reflect on and improve their practice, and take responsibility for identifying and meeting their developing professional needs. (b) Identify priorities for their early professional development in the context of induction.
Q8	Have a creative and constructively critical approach towards innovation, being prepared to adapt their practice where benefits and improvements are identified.
Q9	Act upon advice and feedback and be open to coaching and mentoring.

For free downloads of all these forms go to www.ecmconnections.co.uk

2. Professional knowledge and understanding

Teaching and learning	
Q10	Have a knowledge and understanding of a range of teaching, learning and behaviour management strategies and know how to use and adapt them, including how to personalize learning and provide opportunities for all learners to achieve their potential.
Assessment and monitoring	
Q11	Know the assessment requirements and arrangements for the subjects/curriculum areas they are trained to teach, including those relating to public examinations and qualifications.
Q12	Know a range of approaches to assessment, including the importance of formative assessment.
Q13	Know how to use local and national statistical information to evaluate the effectiveness of their teaching, to monitor the progress of those they teach and to raise levels of attainment.
Subjects and curriculum	
Q14	Have a secure knowledge and understanding of their subjects/curriculum areas and related pedagogy to enable them to teach effectively across the age and ability range for which they are trained.
Q15	Know and understand the relevant statutory and non-statutory curricula and frameworks, including those provided through the National Strategies, for their subjects/curriculum areas, and other relevant initiatives applicable to the age and ability range for which they are trained.
Literacy, numeracy and ICT	
Q16	Have passed the professional skills tests in numeracy, literacy and information and communications technology (ICT).
Q17	Know how to use skills in literacy, numeracy and ICT to support their teaching and wider professional activities.
Achievement and diversity	
Q18	Understand how children and young people develop and how the progress, rate of development and well-being of learners are affected by a range of developmental, social, religious, ethnic, cultural and linguistic influences.
Q19	Know how to make effective personalized provision for those they teach, including those for whom English is an additional language or who have special educational needs or disabilities, and how to take practical account of diversity and promote equality and inclusion in their teaching.
Q20	Know and understand the roles of colleagues with specific responsibilities, including those with responsibility for learners with special educational needs and disabilities and other individual learning needs.
Health and well-being	
Q21	(a) Be aware of the current legal requirements, national policies and guidance on the safeguarding and promotion of the well-being of children and young people. (b) Know how to identify and support children and young people whose progress, development or well-being is affected by changes or difficulties in their personal circumstances, and when to refer them to colleagues for specialist support.

For free downloads of all these forms go to www.ecmconnections.co.uk

3. Professional skills

Planning	
Q22	Plan for progression across the age and ability range for which they are trained, designing effective learning sequences within lessons and across series of lessons and demonstrating secure subject/curriculum knowledge.
Q23	Design opportunities for learners to develop their literacy, numeracy and ICT skills.
Q24	Plan homework or other out-of-class work to sustain learners' progress and to extend and consolidate their learning.

Teaching	
Q25	Teach lessons and sequences of lessons across the age and ability range for which they are trained in which they: (a) use a range of teaching strategies and resources, including e-learning, taking practical account of diversity and promoting equality and inclusion (b) build on prior knowledge, develop concepts and processes, enable learners to apply new knowledge, understanding and skills and meet learning objectives (c) adapt their language to suit the learners they teach, introducing new ideas and concepts clearly, and using explanations, questions, discussions and plenaries effectively (d) demonstrate the ability to manage the learning of individuals, groups and whole classes, modifying their teaching to suit the stage of the lesson.

Assessing, monitoring and giving feedback	
Q26	(a) Make effective use of a range of assessment, monitoring and recording strategies. (b) Assess the learning needs of those they teach in order to set challenging learning objectives.
Q27	Provide timely, accurate and constructive feedback on learners' attainment, progress and areas for development.
Q28	Support and guide learners to reflect on their learning, identify the progress they have made and identify their emerging learning needs.

Reviewing teaching and learning	
Q29	Evaluate the impact of their teaching on the progress of all learners, and modify their planning and classroom practice where necessary.

Learning environment	
Q30	Establish a purposeful and safe learning environment conducive to learning and identify opportunities for learners to learn in out-of-school contexts.
Q31	Establish a clear framework for classroom discipline to manage learners' behaviour constructively and promote their self-control and independence.

Teamworking and collaboration	
Q32	Work as a team member and identify opportunities for working with colleagues, sharing the development of effective practice with them.
Q33	Ensure that colleagues working with them are appropriately involved in supporting learning and understand the roles they are expected to fulfil.

For free downloads of all these forms go to www.ecmconnections.co.uk

Appendix 7: Professional Standards for Teachers – QTS Forms

1. Professional attributes

Relationships with children and young people		Evidence
Q1	Have high expectations of children and young people including a commitment to ensuring that they can achieve their full educational potential and to establishing fair, respectful, trusting, supportive and constructive relationships with them.	
Q2	Demonstrate the positive values, attitudes and behaviour they expect from children and young people.	
Frameworks		**Evidence**
Q3	(a) Be aware of the professional duties of teachers and the statutory framework within which they work. (b) Be aware of the policies and practices of the workplace and share in collective responsibility for their implementation.	
Communicating and working with others		**Evidence**
Q4	Communicate effectively with children, young people, colleagues, parents and carers.	
Q5	Recognize and respect the contribution that colleagues, parents and carers can make to the development and well-being of children and young people, and to raising their levels of attainment.	
Q6	Have a commitment to collaboration and cooperative working.	
Personal professional development		**Evidence**
Q7	(a) Reflect on and improve their practice, and take responsibility for identifying and meeting their developing professional needs. (b) Identify priorities for their early professional development in the context of induction.	
Q8	Have a creative and constructively critical approach towards innovation, being prepared to adapt their practice where benefits and improvements are identified.	
Q9	Act upon advice and feedback and be open to coaching and mentoring.	

For free downloads of all these forms go to www.ecmconnections.co.uk

2. Professional knowledge and understanding

Teaching and learning		Evidence
Q10	Have a knowledge and understanding of a range of teaching, learning and behaviour management strategies and know how to use and adapt them, including how to personalize learning and provide opportunities for all learners to achieve their potential.	
Assessment and monitoring		**Evidence**
Q11	Know the assessment requirements and arrangements for the subjects/curriculum areas they are trained to teach, including those relating to public examinations and qualifications.	
Q12	Know a range of approaches to assessment, including the importance of formative assessment.	
Q13	Know how to use local and national statistical information to evaluate the effectiveness of their teaching, to monitor the progress of those they teach and to raise levels of attainment.	
Subjects and curriculum		**Evidence**
Q14	Have a secure knowledge and understanding of their subjects/curriculum areas and related pedagogy to enable them to teach effectively across the age and ability range for which they are trained.	
Q15	Know and understand the relevant statutory and non-statutory curricula and frameworks, including those provided through the National Strategies, for their subjects/curriculum areas, and other relevant initiatives applicable to the age and ability range for which they are trained.	
Literacy, numeracy and ICT		**Evidence**
Q16	Have passed the professional skills tests in numeracy, literacy and information and communications technology (ICT).	
Q17	Know how to use skills in literacy, numeracy and ICT to support their teaching and wider professional activities.	

For free downloads of all these forms go to www.ecmconnections.co.uk

Achievement and diversity		Evidence
Q18	Understand how children and young people develop and how the progress, rate of development and well-being of learners are affected by a range of developmental, social, religious, ethnic, cultural and linguistic influences.	
Q19	Know how to make effective personalized provision for those they teach, including those for whom English is an additional language or who have special educational needs or disabilities, and how to take practical account of diversity and promote equality and inclusion in their teaching.	
Q20	Know and understand the roles of colleagues with specific responsibilities, including those with responsibility for learners with special educational needs and disabilities and other individual learning needs.	
Health and well-being		Evidence
Q21	(a) Be aware of the current legal requirements, national policies and guidance on the safeguarding and promotion of the well-being of children and young people. (b) Know how to identify and support children and young people whose progress, development or well-being is affected by changes or difficulties in their personal circumstances, and when to refer them to colleagues for specialist support.	

For free downloads of all these forms go to www.ecmconnections.co.uk

3. Professional skills

Planning		Evidence
Q22	Plan for progression across the age and ability range for which they are trained, designing effective learning sequences within lessons and across series of lessons and demonstrating secure subject/ curriculum knowledge.	
Q23	Design opportunities for learners to develop their literacy, numeracy and ICT skills.	
Q24	Plan homework or other out-of-class work to sustain learners' progress and to extend and consolidate their learning.	
Teaching		**Evidence**
Q25	Teach lessons and sequences of lessons across the age and ability range for which they are trained in which they: (a) use a range of teaching strategies and resources, including e-learning, taking practical account of diversity and promoting equality and inclusion (b) build on prior knowledge, develop concepts and processes, enable learners to apply new knowledge, understanding and skills and meet learning objectives (c) adapt their language to suit the learners they teach, introducing new ideas and concepts clearly, and using explanations, questions, discussions and plenaries effectively (d) demonstrate the ability to manage the learning of individuals, groups and whole classes, modifying their teaching to suit the stage of the lesson.	
Assessing, monitoring and giving feedback		**Evidence**
Q26	(a) Make effective use of a range of assessment, monitoring and recording strategies. (b) Assess the learning needs of those they teach in order to set challenging learning objectives.	
Q27	Provide timely, accurate and constructive feedback on learners' attainment, progress and areas for development.	
Q28	Support and guide learners to reflect on their learning, identify the progress they have made and identify their emerging learning needs.	

For free downloads of all these forms go to www.ecmconnections.co.uk

Reviewing teaching and learning		Evidence
Q29	Evaluate the impact of their teaching on the progress of all learners, and modify their planning and classroom practice where necessary.	

Learning environment		Evidence
Q30	Establish a purposeful and safe learning environment conducive to learning and identify opportunities for learners to learn in out-of-school contexts.	
Q31	Establish a clear framework for classroom discipline to manage learners' behaviour constructively and promote their self-control and independence.	

Team-working and collaboration		Evidence
Q32	Work as a team member and identify opportunities for working with colleagues, sharing the development of effective practice with them.	
Q33	Ensure that colleagues working with them are appropriately involved in supporting learning and understand the roles they are expected to fulfil.	

For free downloads of all these forms go to www.ecmconnections.co.uk

Appendix 8: Professional Standards for Teachers – CORE Criteria

1. Professional attributes

Relationships with children and young people	
C1	Have high expectations of children and young people including a commitment to ensuring that they can achieve their full educational potential and to establishing fair, respectful, trusting, supportive and constructive relationships with them.
C2	Hold positive values and attitudes and adopt high standards of behaviour in their professional role.
Frameworks	
C3	Maintain an up-to-date knowledge and understanding of the professional duties of teachers and the statutory framework within which they work, and contribute to the development, implementation and evaluation of the policies and practice of their workplace, including those designed to promote equality of opportunity.
Communicating and working with others	
C4	(a) Communicate effectively with children, young people and colleagues. (b) Communicate effectively with parents and carers, conveying timely and relevant information about attainment, objectives, progress and well-being. (c) Recognize that communication is a two-way process and encourage parents and carers to participate in discussions about the progress, development and well-being of children and young people.
C5	Recognize and respect the contributions that colleagues, parents and carers can make to the development and well-being of children and young people, and to raising their levels of attainment.
C6	Have a commitment to collaboration and co-operative working, where appropriate.
Personal professional development	
C7	Evaluate their performance and be committed to improving their practice through appropriate professional development.
C8	Have a creative and constructively critical approach towards innovation; being prepared to adapt their practice where benefits and improvements are identified.
C9	Act upon advice and feedback and be open to coaching and mentoring.

For free downloads of all these forms go to www.ecmconnections.co.uk

2. Professional knowledge and understanding

Teaching and learning	
C10	Have a good, up-to-date working knowledge and understanding of a range of teaching, learning and behaviour management strategies and know how to use and adapt them, including how to personalize learning to provide opportunities for all learners to achieve their potential.
Assessment and monitoring	
C11	Know the assessment requirements and arrangements for the subjects/curriculum areas they teach, including those relating to public examinations and qualifications.
C12	Know a range of approaches to assessment, including the importance of formative assessment.
C13	Know how to use local and national statistical information to evaluate the effectiveness of their teaching, to monitor the progress of those they teach and to raise levels of attainment.
C14	Know how to use reports and other sources of external information related to assessment in order to provide learners with accurate and constructive feedback on their strengths, weaknesses, attainment, progress and areas for development, including action plans for improvement.
Subjects and curriculum	
C15	Have a secure knowledge and understanding of their subjects/curriculum areas and related pedagogy including: the contribution that their subjects/curriculum areas can make to cross-curricular learning; and recent relevant developments.
C16	Know and understand the relevant statutory and non-statutory curricula and frameworks, including those provided through the National Strategies, for their subjects/curriculum areas and other relevant initiatives across the age and ability range they teach.
Literacy, numeracy and ICT	
C17	Know how to use skills in literacy, numeracy and ICT to support their teaching and wider professional activities.
Achievement and diversity	
C18	Understand how children and young people develop and how the progress, rate of development and well-being of learners are affected by a range of developmental, social, religious, ethnic, cultural and linguistic influences.
C19	Know how to make effective personalized provision for those they teach, including those for whom English is an additional language or who have special educational needs or disabilities, and how to take practical account of diversity and promote equality and inclusion in their teaching.
C20	Understand the roles of colleagues such as those having specific responsibilities for learners with special educational needs, disabilities and other individual learning needs, and the contributions they can make to the learning, development and well-being of children and young people.
C21	Know when to draw on the expertise of colleagues, such as those with responsibility for the safeguarding of children and young people with special educational needs and disabilities, and to refer to sources of information, advice and support from external agencies.

For free downloads of all these forms go to www.ecmconnections.co.uk

Effective Teachers in Secondary Schools

Health and well-being	
C22	Know the current legal requirements, national policies and guidance on the safeguarding and promotion of the well-being of children and young people.
C23	Know the local arrangements concerning the safeguarding of children and young people.
C24	Know how to identify potential child abuse or neglect and follow safeguarding procedures.
C25	Know how to identify and support children and young people whose progress, development or well-being is affected by changes or difficulties in their personal circumstances, and when to refer them to colleagues for specialist support.

For free downloads of all these forms go to www.ecmconnections.co.uk

3. Professional skills

Planning	
C26	Plan for progression across the age and ability range they teach, designing effective learning sequences within lessons and across series of lessons informed by secure subject/curriculum knowledge.
C27	Design opportunities for learners to develop their literacy, numeracy, ICT and thinking and learning skills appropriate within their phase and context.
C28	Plan, set and assess homework, other out-of-class assignments and coursework for examinations, where appropriate, to sustain learners' progress and to extend and consolidate their learning.
Teaching	
C29	Teach challenging, well-organized lessons and sequences of lessons across the age and ability range they teach in which they: (a) use an appropriate range of teaching strategies and resources, including e-learning, which meet learners' needs and take practical account of diversity and promote equality and inclusion (b) build on the prior knowledge and attainment of those they teach in order that learners meet learning objectives and make sustained progress (c) develop concepts and processes which enable learners to apply new knowledge, understanding and skills (d) adapt their language to suit the learners they teach, introducing new ideas and concepts clearly, and using explanations, questions, discussions and plenaries effectively (e) manage the learning of individuals, groups and whole classes effectively, modifying their teaching appropriately to suit the stage of the lesson and the needs of the learners.
C30	Teach engaging and motivating lessons informed by well-grounded expectations of learners and designed to raise levels of attainment.
Assessing, monitoring and giving feedback	
C31	Make effective use of an appropriate range of observation, assessment, monitoring and recording strategies as a basis for setting challenging learning objectives and monitoring learners' progress and levels of attainment.
C32	Provide learners, colleagues, parents and carers with timely, accurate and constructive feedback on learners' attainment, progress and areas for development.
C33	Support and guide learners so that they can reflect on their learning, identify the progress they have made, set positive targets for improvement and become successful independent learners.
C34	Use assessment as part of their teaching to diagnose learners' needs, set realistic and challenging targets for improvement and plan future teaching.
Reviewing teaching and learning	
C35	Review the effectiveness of their teaching and its impact on learners' progress, attainment and well-being, refining their approaches where necessary.
C36	Review the impact of the feedback provided to learners and guide learners on how to improve their attainment.

For free downloads of all these forms go to www.ecmconnections.co.uk

Effective Teachers in Secondary Schools

Learning environment	
C37	(a) Establish a purposeful and safe learning environment which complies with current legal requirements, national policies and guidance on the safeguarding and well-being of children and young people so that learners feel secure and sufficiently confident to make an active contribution to learning and to the school. (b) Make use of the local arrangements concerning the safeguarding of children and young people. (c) Identify and use opportunities to personalize and extend learning through out-of-school contexts where possible making links between in-school learning and learning in out-of-school contexts.
C38	(a) Manage learners' behaviour constructively by establishing and maintaining a clear and positive framework for discipline, in line with the school's behaviour policy. (b) Use a range of behaviour management techniques and strategies, adapting them as necessary to promote the self-control and independence of learners.
C39	Promote learners' self-control, independence and cooperation through developing their social, emotional and behavioural skills.
Team working and collaboration	
C40	Work as a team member and identify opportunities for working with colleagues, managing their work where appropriate and sharing the development of effective practice with them.
C41	Ensure that colleagues working with them are appropriately involved in supporting learning and understand the roles they are expected to fulfil.

For free downloads of all these forms go to www.ecmconnections.co.uk

Appendix 9: Professional Standards for Teachers – CORE Forms

1. Professional attributes

Relationships with children and young people		Evidence
C1	Have high expectations of children and young people including a commitment to ensuring that they can achieve their full educational potential and to establishing fair, respectful, trusting, supportive and constructive relationships with them.	
C2	Hold positive values and attitudes and adopt high standards of behaviour in their professional role	
Frameworks		**Evidence**
C3	Maintain an up-to-date knowledge and understanding of the professional duties of teachers and the statutory framework within which they work, and contribute to the development, implementation and evaluation of the policies and practice of their workplace, including those designed to promote equality of opportunity.	
Communicating and working with others		**Evidence**
C4	(a) Communicate effectively with children, young people and colleagues. (b) Communicate effectively with parents and carers, conveying timely and relevant information about attainment, objectives, progress and well-being. (c) Recognize that communication is a two-way process and encourage parents and carers to participate in discussions about the progress, development and well-being of children and young people.	
C5	Recognize and respect the contributions that colleagues, parents and carers can make to the development and well-being of children and young people, and to raising their levels of attainment.	
C6	Have a commitment to collaboration and co-operative working, where appropriate.	
Personal professional development		**Evidence**
C7	Evaluate their performance and be committed to improving their practice through appropriate professional development.	
C8	Have a creative and constructively critical approach towards innovation; being prepared to adapt their practice where benefits and improvements are identified.	
C9	Act upon advice and feedback and be open to coaching and mentoring.	

For free downloads of all these forms go to www.ecmconnections.co.uk

2. Professional knowledge and understanding

Teaching and learning		Evidence
C10	Have a good, up-to-date working knowledge and understanding of a range of teaching, learning and behaviour management strategies and know how to use and adapt them, including how to personalize learning to provide opportunities for all learners to achieve their potential.	
Assessment and monitoring		**Evidence**
C11	Know the assessment requirements and arrangements for the subjects/curriculum areas they teach, including those relating to public examinations and qualifications.	
C12	Know a range of approaches to assessment, including the importance of formative assessment.	
C13	Know how to use local and national statistical information to evaluate the effectiveness of their teaching, to monitor the progress of those they teach and to raise levels of attainment.	
C14	Know how to use reports and other sources of external information related to assessment in order to provide learners with accurate and constructive feedback on their strengths, weaknesses, attainment, progress and areas for development, including action plans for improvement.	
Subjects and curriculum		**Evidence**
C15	Have a secure knowledge and understanding of their subjects/ curriculum areas and related pedagogy including: the contribution that their subjects/curriculum areas can make to cross-curricular learning; and recent relevant developments.	
C16	Know and understand the relevant statutory and non-statutory curricula and frameworks, including those provided through the National Strategies, for their subjects/curriculum areas and other relevant initiatives across the age and ability range they teach.	
Literacy, numeracy and ICT		**Evidence**
C17	Know how to use skills in literacy, numeracy and ICT to support their teaching and wider professional activities.	
Achievement and diversity		**Evidence**
C18	Understand how children and young people develop and how the progress, rate of development and well-being of learners are affected by a range of developmental, social, religious, ethnic, cultural and linguistic influences.	

For free downloads of all these forms go to www.ecmconnections.co.uk

C19	Know how to make effective personalized provision for those they teach, including those for whom English is an additional language or who have special educational needs or disabilities, and how to take practical account of diversity and promote equality and inclusion in their teaching.	
C20	Understand the roles of colleagues such as those having specific responsibilities for learners with special educational needs, disabilities and other individual learning needs, and the contributions they can make to the learning, development and well-being of children and young people.	
C21	Know when to draw on the expertise of colleagues, such as those with responsibility for the safeguarding of children and young people with special educational needs and disabilities, and to refer to sources of information, advice and support from external agencies.	
Health and well-being		**Evidence**
C22	Know the current legal requirements, national policies and guidance on the safeguarding and promotion of the well-being of children and young people.	
C23	Know the local arrangements concerning the safeguarding of children and young people.	
C24	Know how to identify potential child abuse or neglect and follow safeguarding procedures.	
C25	Know how to identify and support children and young people whose progress, development or well-being is affected by changes or difficulties in their personal circumstances, and when to refer them to colleagues for specialist support.	

For free downloads of all these forms go to www.ecmconnections.co.uk

3. Professional skills

Planning		Evidence
C26	Plan for progression across the age and ability range they teach, designing effective learning sequences within lessons and across series of lessons informed by secure subject/curriculum knowledge.	
C27	Design opportunities for learners to develop their literacy, numeracy, ICT and thinking and learning skills appropriate within their phase and context.	
C28	Plan, set and assess homework, other out-of-class assignments and coursework for examinations, where appropriate, to sustain learners' progress and to extend and consolidate their learning.	
Teaching		**Evidence**
C29	Teach challenging, well-organized lessons and sequences of lessons across the age and ability range they teach in which they: (a) use an appropriate range of teaching strategies and resources, including e-learning, which meet learners' needs and take practical account of diversity and promote equality and inclusion (b) build on the prior knowledge and attainment of those they teach in order that learners meet learning objectives and make sustained progress (c) develop concepts and processes which enable learners to apply new knowledge, understanding and skills (d) adapt their language to suit the learners they teach, introducing new ideas and concepts clearly, and using explanations, questions, discussions and plenaries effectively (e) manage the learning of individuals, groups and whole classes effectively, modifying their teaching appropriately to suit the stage of the lesson and the needs of the learners.	
C30	Teach engaging and motivating lessons informed by well-grounded expectations of learners and designed to raise levels of attainment.	
Assessing, monitoring and giving feedback		**Evidence**
C31	Make effective use of an appropriate range of observation, assessment, monitoring and recording strategies as a basis for setting challenging learning objectives and monitoring learners' progress and levels of attainment.	

For free downloads of all these forms go to www.ecmconnections.co.uk

C32	Provide learners, colleagues, parents and carers with timely, accurate and constructive feedback on learners' attainment, progress and areas for development.	
C33	Support and guide learners so that they can reflect on their learning, identify the progress they have made, set positive targets for improvement and become successful independent learners.	
C34	Use assessment as part of their teaching to diagnose learners' needs, set realistic and challenging targets for improvement and plan future teaching.	
Reviewing teaching and learning		**Evidence**
C35	Review the effectiveness of their teaching and its impact on learners' progress, attainment and well-being, refining their approaches where necessary.	
C36	Review the impact of the feedback provided to learners and guide learners on how to improve their attainment.	
Learning environment		**Evidence**
C37	(a) Establish a purposeful and safe learning environment which complies with current legal requirements, national policies and guidance on the safeguarding and well-being of children and young people so that learners feel secure and sufficiently confident to make an active contribution to learning and to the school. (b) Make use of the local arrangements concerning the safeguarding of children and young people. (c) Identify and use opportunities to personalize and extend learning through out-of-school contexts where possible making links between in-school learning and learning in out-of-school contexts.	
C38	(a) Manage learners' behaviour constructively by establishing and maintaining a clear and positive framework for discipline, in line with the school's behaviour policy. (b) Use a range of behaviour management techniques and strategies, adapting them as necessary to promote the self-control and independence of learners.	
C39	Promote learners' self-control, independence and cooperation through developing their social, emotional and behavioural skills.	

For free downloads of all these forms go to www.ecmconnections.co.uk

Teamworking and collaboration		Evidence
C40	Work as a team member and identify opportunities for working with colleagues, managing their work where appropriate and sharing the development of effective practice with them.	
C41	Ensure that colleagues working with them are appropriately involved in supporting learning and understand the roles they are expected to fulfil.	

For free downloads of all these forms go to www.ecmconnections.co.uk

Appendix 10: Professional Standards for Teachers – Post Threshold Criteria

1. Professional attributes

Relationships with children and young people	
Frameworks	
P1	Contribute significantly, where appropriate, to implementing workplace policies and practice and to promoting collective responsibility for their implementation.
Communicating and working with others	
Personal professional development	

For free downloads of all these forms go to www.ecmconnections.co.uk

2. Professional knowledge and understanding

Teaching and learning	
P2	Have an extensive knowledge and understanding of how to use and adapt a range of teaching, learning and behaviour management strategies, including how to personalize learning to provide opportunities for all learners to achieve their potential.
Assessment and monitoring	
P3	Have an extensive knowledge and well-informed understanding of the assessment requirements and arrangements for the subjects/curriculum areas they teach, including those related to public examinations and qualifications.
P4	Have up-to-date knowledge and understanding of the different types of qualification and specification and their suitability for meeting learners' needs.
Subjects and curriculum	
P5	Have a more developed knowledge and understanding of their subjects/curriculum areas and related pedagogy including how learning progresses within them.
Literacy, numeracy and ICT	
Achievement and diversity	
Health and well-being	
P6	Have sufficient depth of knowledge and experience to be able to give advice on the development and well-being of children and young people.

For free downloads of all these forms go to www.ecmconnections.co.uk

3. Professional skills

Planning	
P7	Be flexible, creative and adept at designing learning sequences within lessons and across lessons that are effective and consistently well-matched to learning objectives and the needs of learners, and which integrate recent developments, including those relating to subject/curriculum knowledge.
Teaching	
P8	Have teaching skills that lead to learners achieving well relative to their prior attainment, making progress as good as, or better than, similar learners nationally.
Assessing, monitoring and giving feedback	
Reviewing teaching and learning	
Learning environment	
Teamworking and collaboration	
P9	Promote collaboration and work effectively as a team member.
P10	Contribute to the professional development of colleagues through coaching and mentoring, demonstrating effective practice, and providing advice and feedback.

For free downloads of all these forms go to www.ecmconnections.co.uk

Appendix 11: Professional Standards for Teachers – Post Threshold Forms

1. Professional attributes

Relationships with children and young people	
Frameworks	**Evidence**
P1	Contribute significantly, where appropriate, to implementing workplace policies and practice and to promoting collective responsibility for their implementation.	
Communicating and working with others	
Personal professional development	

For free downloads of all these forms go to www.ecmconnections.co.uk

2. Professional knowledge and understanding

Teaching and learning		Evidence
P2	Have an extensive knowledge and understanding of how to use and adapt a range of teaching, learning and behaviour management strategies, including how to personalize learning to provide opportunities for all learners to achieve their potential.	
Assessment and monitoring		**Evidence**
P3	Have an extensive knowledge and well-informed understanding of the assessment requirements and arrangements for the subjects/curriculum areas they teach, including those related to public examinations and qualifications.	
P4	Have up-to-date knowledge and understanding of the different types of qualification and specification and their suitability for meeting learners' needs.	
Subjects and curriculum		**Evidence**
P5	Have a more developed knowledge and understanding of their subjects/curriculum areas and related pedagogy including how learning progresses within them.	
Literacy, numeracy and ICT		
Achievement and diversity		
Health and well-being		**Evidence**
P6	Have sufficient depth of knowledge and experience to be able to give advice on the development and well-being of children and young people.	

For free downloads of all these forms go to www.ecmconnections.co.uk

3. Professional skills

Planning		Evidence
P7	Be flexible, creative and adept at designing learning sequences within lessons and across lessons that are effective and consistently well-matched to learning objectives and the needs of learners, and which integrate recent developments, including those relating to subject/curriculum knowledge.	
Teaching		**Evidence**
P8	Have teaching skills that lead to learners achieving well relative to their prior attainment, making progress as good as, or better than, similar learners nationally.	
Assessing, monitoring and giving feedback		
Reviewing teaching and learning		
Learning environment		
Team working and collaboration		**Evidence**
P9	Promote collaboration and work effectively as a team member.	
P10	Contribute to the professional development of colleagues through coaching and mentoring, demonstrating effective practice, and providing advice and feedback.	

For free downloads of all these forms go to www.ecmconnections.co.uk

Appendix 12: Professional Standards for Teachers – Excellent Teacher Criteria

1. Professional attributes

Relationships with children and young people	
Frameworks	
E1	Be willing to take a leading role in developing workplace policies and practice and in promoting collective responsibility for their implementation.
Communicating and working with others	
Personal professional development	
E2	Research and evaluate innovative curricular practices and draw on research outcomes and other sources of external evidence to inform their own practice and that of colleagues.

For free downloads of all these forms go to www.ecmconnections.co.uk

2. Professional knowledge and understanding

Teaching and learning	
E3	Have a critical understanding of the most effective teaching, learning and behaviour management strategies, including how to select and use approaches that personalize learning to provide opportunities for all learners to achieve their potential.
Assessment and monitoring	
E4	Know how to improve the effectiveness of assessment practice in the workplace, including how to analyse statistical information to evaluate the effectiveness of teaching and learning across the school.
Subjects and curriculum	
E5	Have an extensive and deep knowledge and understanding of their subjects/curriculum areas and related pedagogy gained, for example, through involvement in wider professional networks associated with their subjects/curriculum areas.
Literacy, numeracy and ICT	
Achievement and diversity	
E6	Have an extensive knowledge on matters concerning equality, inclusion and diversity in teaching.
Health and well-being	

For free downloads of all these forms go to www.ecmconnections.co.uk

3. Professional skills

Planning	
E7	(a) Take a lead in planning collaboratively with colleagues in order to promote effective practice. (b) Identify and explore links within and between subjects/curriculum areas in their planning.
Teaching	
E8	Have teaching skills that lead to excellent results and outcomes.
E9	Demonstrate excellent and innovative pedagogical practice.
Assessing, monitoring and giving feedback	
E10	Demonstrate excellent ability to assess and evaluate.
E11	Have an excellent ability to provide learners, colleagues, parents and carers with timely, accurate and constructive feedback on learners' attainment, progress and areas for development that promotes pupil progress.
Reviewing teaching and learning	
E12	Use local and national statistical data and other information, in order to provide: (a) a comparative baseline for evaluating learners' progress and attainment (b) a means of judging the effectiveness of their teaching, and (c) a basis for improving teaching and learning.
Learning environment	
Teamworking and collaboration	
E13	Work closely with leadership teams, taking a leading role in developing, implementing and evaluating policies and practice that contribute to school improvement.
E14	Contribute to the professional development of colleagues using a broad range of techniques and skills appropriate to their needs so that they demonstrate enhanced and effective practice.
E15	Make well-founded appraisals of situations upon which they are asked to advise, applying high level skills in classroom observation to evaluate and advise colleagues on their work and devising and implementing effective strategies to meet the learning needs of children and young people leading to improvements in pupil outcomes.

For free downloads of all these forms go to www.ecmconnections.co.uk

Appendix 13: Professional Standards for Teachers – Excellent Teacher Forms

1. Professional attributes

Relationships with children and young people		
Frameworks		**Evidence**
E1	Be willing to take a leading role in developing workplace policies and practice and in promoting collective responsibility for their implementation.	
Communicating and working with others		
Personal professional development		**Evidence**
E2	Research and evaluate innovative curricular practices and draw on research outcomes and other sources of external evidence to inform their own practice and that of colleagues.	

For free downloads of all these forms go to www.ecmconnections.co.uk

2. Professional knowledge and understanding

Teaching and learning		Evidence
E3	Have a critical understanding of the most effective teaching, learning and behaviour management strategies, including how to select and use approaches that personalize learning to provide opportunities for all learners to achieve their potential.	
Assessment and monitoring		**Evidence**
E4	Know how to improve the effectiveness of assessment practice in the workplace, including how to analyse statistical information to evaluate the effectiveness of teaching and learning across the school.	
Subjects and curriculum		**Evidence**
E5	Have an extensive and deep knowledge and understanding of their subjects/curriculum areas and related pedagogy gained, for example, through involvement in wider professional networks associated with their subjects/curriculum areas.	
Literacy, numeracy and ICT		
Achievement and diversity		**Evidence**
E6	Have an extensive knowledge on matters concerning equality, inclusion and diversity in teaching.	
Health and well-being		

For free downloads of all these forms go to www.ecmconnections.co.uk

3. Professional skills

Planning		Evidence
E7	(a) Take a lead in planning collaboratively with colleagues in order to promote effective practice. (b) Identify and explore links within and between subjects/curriculum areas in their planning.	
Teaching		**Evidence**
E8	Have teaching skills that lead to excellent results and outcomes.	
E9	Demonstrate excellent and innovative pedagogical practice.	
Assessing, monitoring and giving feedback		**Evidence**
E10	Demonstrate excellent ability to assess and evaluate.	
E11	Have an excellent ability to provide learners, colleagues, parents and carers with timely, accurate and constructive feedback on learners' attainment, progress and areas for development that promotes pupil progress.	
Reviewing teaching and learning		**Evidence**
E12	Use local and national statistical data and other information, in order to provide: (a) a comparative baseline for evaluating learners' progress and attainment (b) a means of judging the effectiveness of their teaching, and (c) a basis for improving teaching and learning.	
Learning environment		
Teamworking and collaboration		**Evidence**
E13	Work closely with leadership teams, taking a leading role in developing, implementing and evaluating policies and practice that contribute to school improvement.	
E14	Contribute to the professional development of colleagues using a broad range of techniques and skills appropriate to their needs so that they demonstrate enhanced and effective practice.	

For free downloads of all these forms go to www.ecmconnections.co.uk

| E15 | Make well-founded appraisals of situations upon which they are asked to advise, applying high level skills in classroom observation to evaluate and advise colleagues on their work and devising and implementing effective strategies to meet the learning needs of children and young people leading to improvements in pupil outcomes. | |

For free downloads of all these forms go to www.ecmconnections.co.uk

Appendix 14: Professional Standards for Teachers – Advanced Skills Teacher Criteria

1. Professional attributes

Relationships with children and young people	
Frameworks	
A1	Be willing to take on a strategic leadership role in developing workplace policies and practice and in promoting collective responsibility for their implementation in their own and other workplaces.
Communicating and working with others	
Personal professional development	

For free downloads of all these forms go to www.ecmconnections.co.uk

2. Professional knowledge and understanding

Teaching and learning

Assessment and monitoring

Subjects and curriculum

Literacy, numeracy and ICT

Achievement and diversity

Health and well-being

For free downloads of all these forms go to www.ecmconnections.co.uk

3. Professional skills

Planning	
Teaching	
Assessing, monitoring and giving feedback	
Reviewing teaching and learning	
Learning environment	
Teamworking and collaboration	
A2	Be part of or work closely with leadership teams, taking a leadership role in developing, implementing and evaluating policies and practice in their own and other workplaces that contribute to school improvement.
A3	Possess the analytical, interpersonal and organizational skills necessary to work effectively with staff and leadership teams beyond their own school.

For free downloads of all these forms go to www.ecmconnections.co.uk

Appendix 15: Professional Standards for Teachers – Advanced Skills Teacher Forms

1. Professional attributes

Relationships with children and young people	
Frameworks	**Evidence**
A1	Be willing to take on a strategic leadership role in developing workplace policies and practice and in promoting collective responsibility for their implementation in their own and other workplaces.	
Communicating and working with others	
Personal professional development	

For free downloads of all these forms go to www.ecmconnections.co.uk

2. Professional knowledge and understanding

Teaching and learning	
Assessment and monitoring	
Subjects and curriculum	
Literacy, numeracy and ICT	
Achievement and diversity	
Health and well-being	

For free downloads of all these forms go to www.ecmconnections.co.uk

3. Professional skills

Planning	
Teaching	
Assessing, monitoring and giving feedback	
Reviewing teaching and learning	
Learning environment	
Teamworking and collaboration	**Evidence**
A2	Be part of or work closely with leadership teams, taking a leadership role in developing, implementing and evaluating policies and practice in their own and other workplaces that contribute to school improvement.	
A3	Possess the analytical, interpersonal and organizational skills necessary to work effectively with staff and leadership teams beyond their own school.	

For free downloads of all these forms go to www.ecmconnections.co.uk

Appendix 16: Threshold Application Forms

EXAMPLE 1: A COMPLETED THRESHOLD ASSESSMENT APPLICATION FORM

IMPORTANT: PLEASE READ THE ENCLOSED GUIDANCE NOTES BEFORE STARTING TO COMPLETE THE APPLICATION FORM.

THIS APPLICATION FORM SHOULD BE HANDLED IN CONFIDENCE AT ALL TIMES.

Access to this form will be restricted to those who are playing a part in the assessment and verification process.

Personal Details

Surname: First Name(s):

Home Address/Telephone/e:mail/fax:

DfEE/Wesh Office Teacher Reference Number:

Career Details

Current post:

Date joined present school: Length in Post:

If not in school, current post and last teaching post (please give dates)

Subject or area specialism, if relevant:

Name and Location of School (or other employer):

Name of head:

Primary   Secondary   Other

Equal Opportunities Monitoring

The DfEE is committed to equal opportunities. We would like to monitor the profile of those applying for threshold assessment and the outcomes.

To enable us to do this, please complete the enclosed equal opportunities questionnaire and pass it to your headteacher who will forward it with your application form. The information you give us will be treated as confidential and will not form part of the application process.

Data Protection Act 1998

The Department for Education and Employment will process the information collected in this document for the purpose of assessing and monitoring teachers' applications to cross the performance threshold. This information will be processed only within the terms of the Department's Data Protection notification.

1. KNOWLEDGE AND UNDERSTANDING

Please summarise evidence that you:

- **have a thorough and up-to-date knowledge of the teaching of your subject(s) and take account of wider curriculum developments which are relevant to your work.**

A. I have a sound and up-to-date knowledge of good teaching techniques and how these can be used in my own subject and in teaching in general.
- I have personally devised a project that I will be working on this coming year in Leeds. (A copy of the project is available in my portfolio.)
- I have worked closely with Mr D (from the Raising Achievement Division in Leeds) and will continue to do so this coming year.
- I have, over the past year, visited a number of schools in Leeds to observe effective classroom practitioners.
- I have organised a highly successful training morning (on May 19th 2000) for 15 staff at the school, bringing in Mrs E to introduce the thinking skills developed by Edward de Bono.

B. I know my subject in sufficient depth to teach effectively.
- I always incorporate into lessons examples of how physics is of relevance in the world around us through personal examples if possible. For example, how ultrasound was used to scan my children before they were born (I bring in the photographs I have from these scans), or how radioactive materials have been used to treat cancer.
- I have studied, as part of an MEd at the University of Leeds, how children learn concepts in science. This has made me particularly aware of the concepts which children bring with them to lessons and how these are only to a certain extent modified by the "science" which they are taught. (My detailed views on this are in my portfolio.)
- I have helped the HoD in Physics to develop the schemes of work and added worksheets and tests which are used by the whole department.
- I use "Egg Races" (last year with Year 7 and previously with Year 9) and SATIS to stimulate students. (Copies of SATIS I have used are in my office.)
- I successfully and confidently teach students across the whole age range from Year 7 to the upper sixth.

C. I have a broad experience of teaching in a number of secondary schools.
- 4 years of teaching at C School, 11 years of teaching at F School and 3 years of teaching at G School. This has enabled me to see and study a broad range of effective teaching styles.

D. I am interested in and aware of national strategies relevant to my teaching and work as a Head of Key Stage 4.
- Through my work as a governor at my own children's primary school – the literacy and numeracy strategies have had a great impact here and this impact will influence the work we do in secondary schools. I consider that introducing pupils to the specific language of physics and the application of number work in real situations is a key part of my work.
- Through serving on the Academic Board in C School.
- Through serving on the SEN committee.

Assessment by headteacher, noting any areas for further development.

Standard Met/Not Yet Met

Effective Teachers in Secondary Schools

2. TEACHING AND ASSESSMENT

Please summarise evidence that you consistently and effectively:

• **plan lessons and sequences of lessons to meet pupils' individual learning needs**

A. I use a personally devised 'Lesson Planning Sheet' to ensure continuity in my lessons and to target individuals and groups.
• These incorporate references to the SoWs.
• They also break the structure of the lessons down into activity-segments, which are given time allocations.
• Classroom and homework sheets and other references from texts are given.
• The framework which this gives is flexibly used within the lesson to allow for the development of work and questions which any individual class can bring to the lesson.

(Example of this in my portfolio.)

B. I communicate learning objectives clearly to pupils.
• I give the pupils a summary of what they are to learn during the course of the lesson at the start of the lesson (I often ask pupils to write this in their books).

(A copy of a page from a typical pupil's book is in my prepared portfolio.)
• At the end of the lesson I summarise what has been learnt myself or ask pupils to do this for the class.

C. I make effective use of homework and other opportunities for learning outside the classroom.
• I set exercises where the pupils have to find information out for themselves (including using Encarta and other reference sources).
• I set homeworks which are differentiated and allow students to investigate topics to varying degrees.
(Examples of these homework points in my portfolio.)

D. I have built up over my teaching career a set of files which incorporate all the work for each section of the GCSE and 'A' level syllabuses.
• These include worksheets and question sheets.
• They also include experimental exercises and additional information from a number of sources. *(These files are readily available for inspection in my office.)*

• **use a range of appropriate strategies for teaching and classroom management**

A. I have a good understanding of the most effective lesson structures, classroom teaching strategies and methods of motivating pupils.
• I have read a number of recent publications (and watched videos) concerning good teaching practice and new ideas. (e.g. *Accelerated Learning in the Classroom* by Alistair Smith, *Closing the Learning Gap* by Mike Hughes, *Succeeding with Difficult Pupils* by Lee Cantor, training videos by Bill Rogers and Robert Powell.)
• This coming year I will be carrying out a project in Leeds with the Raising Achievement Division. (A copy of the project is available in my portfolio.)
• I regularly use mind-map techniques and acrostics in my classroom to encourage learning. I also regularly use pair-work, group-work and brainstorming techniques to complement the traditional format of science lessons. My view is that this enables more pupils of varying abilities and gender to access the concepts in physics. (The Head of Science is aware of these strategies I use.)

B. I always encourage and support pupils by giving positive feedback at all times whilst dealing with examples of misbehaviour promptly and effectively.
• Verbally in the classroom I praise, encourage and raise pupils' self-esteem and confidence by the very good rapport I establish with them.
• I use personally created 'stickers' in the books of pupils. (Copies of these 'stickers' are available in my portfolio.)
• I create a safe classroom environment where mutual respect is an essential element. In my work as Head of KS4 I also insist on positive behaviour at all times.

C. I am aware of the semiotics of the classroom environment and its influence on learning and I use this as a positive learning tool.
• I believe the way a teacher dresses sets a tone and atmosphere and I always dress in a smart and business-like fashion.
• The use of music and a variety of teaching approaches (mentioned above) once again helps me to establish an environment which accommodates the predominant aural, visual or kinaesthetic learning styles of individual pupils. (The Head of Science is aware of my use of music.)

2. TEACHING AND ASSESSMENT (CONTINUED)

Please summarise evidence that you consistently and effectively:

- **use information about prior attainment to set well-grounded expectations for pupils and monitor progress to give clear and constructive feedback.**

A. I always use my knowledge of pupils' individual learning needs to plan lessons and sequences of lessons (and thereby to target individual pupils and groups to ensure good year-on-year progression).
- I change my lesson plans when necessary to accommodate the individual needs and responses of pupils during the course of the lessons.
- I use extension tasks for the most able. (My worksheets demonstrate this and are available in my office for observation.)
- The progress and transition of pupils from one year to another is discussed during departmental meetings.
- I analyse the results of the pupils I teach to ensure that they are on or above the targets previously set for them.
- I use the information supplied by the SEN department concerning pupils on the Leeds Matrix together with IEP's to accommodate pupils with individual learning needs in my lesson plans. I keep the Leeds Matrix information in my office and the IEPs of pupils I teach in my teaching file.

B. I report clearly and in detail to parents and pupils concerning attainment and effort.
- I consider and use the school reporting process as a vital tool to inform parents about the progress of their son/daughter in addition to the feedback I provide on an ongoing basis verbally.
- I set and mark homework regularly and I feed back to pupils detailed information in their exercise books based on departmental marking policies, coupled with individual and personal guidance for improvement. *(Copies of homework are in my portfolio.)*

C. As the Head of Key Stage 4 I report to parents concerning the achievement of their son/daughter.
- I send positive letters home to parents when I have analysed the production of interim and final reports from teachers, and also when pupils carry out difficult tasks such as reading in assemblies. (Copies of typical letters are in my portfolio.)
- The letters following reports are based on the effort (and attainment within their ability range) of pupils rather than just their achievement in subjects.

(Evidence of the effectiveness of the letters I send home and how well-received they are by parents is available from Mr G, the Deputy Headteacher.)

Assessment by headteacher, noting any areas for further development. Each of the three standards above must be met.

Standard Met/Not Yet Met

3. PUPIL PROGRESS

Please summarise evidence that **as a result of your teaching your pupils achieve well relative to their prior attainment, making progress as good or better than similar pupils nationally. This should be shown in marks or grades in any relevant national tests or examinations, or school based assessment for pupils where national tests and examinations are not taken.**

❖ **Class example 1: Year 11 single GCSE science group who took their GCSE in physics in 1999.**
- Actual progress: 13 pupils out of 18 had a positive residual from the information provided in the school by Mr H. That is, 13 pupils achieved better in physics than they did on average in other subjects in the school. Using baseline data and comparing the outcomes at GCSE with CAT predictions none of the pupils I taught achieved a grade lower than was predicted.
- Evaluation of progress: The group had an overall average substantial positive residual of 0.24. This equates to a total positive residual for the group of 4.56 – that is, the group I taught gained over 4.5 GCSE grades in physics more than they did on average in other subjects they took in the school. The CAT data shows that of the 18 pupils in the group 13 achieved a grade in physics above that predicted. In fact the total value-added effect of my teaching was 18 grades improvement for the group above the predicted grades from CATS.

❖ **Class example 2: Year 11 dual award GCSE science group who took their GCSE in science in 1999. (This group was taught by myself and two other teachers – in biology and chemistry.)**
- Actual progress: 13 pupils out of 20 had a positive residual from the information provided in the school by Mr Casey. That is, 13 pupils achieved better in science than they did on average in other subjects in the school. Using baseline data and comparing the outcomes at GCSE with CAT predictions the pupils on the whole achieved grades above those predicted.
- Evaluation of progress: The group had an overall positive residual of 0.49. This equates to a total positive residual for the group of 9.8 – that is the group I taught gained over 9.8 GCSE grades in science more than they did on average in other subjects they took in the school. Two pupils in this group achieved GCSE grades which were two levels above those predicted from the CATS.

The pupils in both the groups above therefore achieved, on average, better than they did in other subjects in the school and better than those grades predicted from CATS. This was the case even though C School pupils achieved extremely well (according to PANDA information provided to the school), above the national average and above the level of comparable schools in 1999.

(Photocopies of the results for both of the classes above, together with the residuals and CAT predictions, are in my portfolio.)

❖ **Class example 3: 'A' level physics group who took their 'A' level in 1999. (This group was taught by myself and one other teacher.)**
- Actual progress: 7 students took a physics 'A' level in 1999. Of these, 3 achieved a top A grade, 1 got a B and 2 got a C.
- Evaluation of progress: 4 of the students achieved 'A' level grades which were well above the grades their GCSE points score suggested. Their total value added 'A' level points score was 7.75 (equivalent to nearly 4 'A' level grades of improvement between the 4 students). The other three students achieved grades only just below their predicted grades from GCSE results.

(Details and analysis of these 'A' level results are in my portfolio.)

Assessment by headteacher, noting any areas for further development.

Standard Met/Not Yet Met

4. WIDER PROFESSIONAL EFFECTIVENESS

Please summarise evidence that you:

- **take responsibility for your professional development and use the outcomes to improve your teaching and pupils' learning**

A. I view it as important to share examples of good classroom management practice in the school.
- This coming year I will be the coordinator of a project in Leeds. This will be supported by Leeds Education Authority and Leeds Metropolitan University. This project has been devised by me and has been developed over the past year.

B. I believe that it is important to give certain pupils additional support which can make a significant difference to their potential examination outcomes.
- I am in charge of the mentoring process involving teachers in my school.
- I also coordinate an external-mentoring scheme involving people from industry mentoring Year 10 pupils.

C. I have arranged a number of additional evenings for parents of Year 9 and Year 7 pupils. This has given me valuable professional development along with other teachers who asked to take part in the evenings.
- These took place for the first time last year in the Summer term and the object was to suggest ways for parents to help their son/daughter with homework, as well as allowing parents to get together and discuss certain issues with each other in an informal environment.
- The attendance was very good with over 100 parents coming along on each of the evenings. *(Copies of booklets I produced for these evenings are available in my portfolio and evidence for the success of these evenings can be gained from Mrs C.)*

D. I am part of a 5-person group (including the Headteacher, a Deputy Headteacher and two senior teachers) which has worked on a bid for Technology College status for the school this coming year.
- If successful, I would be given the responsibility (along with another Senior Teacher) of overseeing the establishment of further links with the community and the development of the bid through rigorous monitoring and evaluation procedures over the next four years.

- **make an active contribution to the policies and aspirations of your school.**

A. I consider that I make a valuable contribution to the school through my work as the Head of Key Stage 4.
- By being a representative for the school in my work with parents.
- By setting a set of guidelines for pupils which will influence their behaviour and conduct in school.
- I have contributed to the school discipline policy, home school agreement, anti-bullying statement and anti-racism statement through the Pastoral Management Group.

B. I believe that in my own teaching it is important to be aware of issues which can influence the learning and development of pupils, and in addition to encourage other teachers to embrace new ideas and good practice.
- As previously stated, through my work on the Technology College bid.
- As previously stated, through my project in Leeds.
- As previously stated, through my broad reading of issues involving good teaching practice.
- As previously stated, through the additional evenings I have developed for parents at C School.
- As previously stated, through the Edward de Bono training morning I organised.

C. I use ICT extensively in my work as a Head of Key Stage.
- A lot of my work concerning the internal exams utilises WORD. *(Evidence available in my office.)*
- I have presented a number of evenings to parents using PowerPoint. ('Options Evening' for parents of Year 9 pupils, 'Into GCSEs Evening' for parents of pupils about to start their GCSEs, and 'Starting Out Evening' for the parents of pupils who have just started at the school.) *(Copies of all of these are available in my portfolio.)*
- I use the Management Information System to Coordinate the options process in Year 9.

D. I believe it is important to emphasise the positive and reward pupils whenever possible.
- I initiated a system of certificates for pupils in Years 10 and 11. Teachers award these to pupils for good work. A record of all certificates received by pupils is kept in the pastoral department and letters of congratulation sent home at key times during the year. Parents have commented very favourably on the system of letters being sent home. *(The Pastoral Deputy Headteacher can verify this and copies of letters sent home are in my portfolio.)*

Assessment by headteacher, noting any areas for further development. Both standards must be met.

Standards Met/Not Yet Met

Effective Teachers in Secondary Schools

5. PROFESSIONAL CHARACTERISTICS

Much of what you have said earlier in this form will give information about the professional characteristics you show in your teaching. Please give any further examples here of how you:

- **challenge and support all pupils to do their best through**

     inspiring trust and confidence
     building team commitment
     engaging and motivating pupils
     analytical thinking
     positive action to improve the quality of pupils' learning.

A. I believe I inspire trust and confidence which enables pupils to work in a secure environment and teachers and parents to have faith in my professional approach.
- I set high standards for pupils in my work as a classroom teacher and as the Head of Key Stage 4.
- I believe that colleagues and pupils view me as an optimistic and positive individual and one who is also approachable, sensitive and supportive.
- I give pupils the freedom and confidence to learn by creating a well structured and caring classroom environment.
- I expect and attain high standards of discipline and behaviour.
- I have always received very positive feedback from parents (e.g. at Parent/Teacher consultation evenings).

B. I build a team commitment with colleagues and pupils.
- One way I do this is through my work as the Head of Key Stage 4 which involves me giving support to the form tutors, classroom teachers and pupils.
- I also do this through my general classroom approach, which emphasises the need for each individual to contribute to the group ethos.

C. I use a variety of opportunities including assemblies to engage and motivate pupils and to set an ethos for pupils built on mutual respect and good manners.
- Teachers and pupils have given me positive feedback following assemblies.
- As a pastoral head, I have worked extremely hard to motivate pupils who are disaffected and often socially excluded.

D. I am constantly aware of the need to use analytical thinking to improve my teaching and the teaching of my colleagues.
- I have a deep interest in looking at the most effective methods of classroom management. (Reading books mentioned earlier such as "Accelerated Learning", the "VITAL" project I have devised, bringing in a representative of Edward de Bono to talk to teachers in the school and part of my new role in school this next year to disseminate good classroom practice.)

E. My teaching techniques have received favourable feedback over a number of years and from a variety of sources but I am constantly aware of the need to improve the quality of pupils' learning.
- I received a "Distinction" in my early days of teaching during my PGCE teaching practice.
- Recently my OFSTED grades were very positive.
- Feedback from Mrs J, Headteacher, has been encouraging.

Assessment by headteacher, taking account of each aspect above and noting any areas for further development.

Standard Met/Not Yet Met

Declaration by applicant

I certify that I am eligible for assessment and that the information in this form is correct. I would like the evidence I have presented to be taken into account in assessing my work against the threshold standards. I understand that further pay progression on the upper pay range will be awarded on the basis of performance and accept that my annual reviews will be used to inform such judgements.

Signed ....   Date ....

Declaration by headteacher (or equivalent if not in school)

Applicant name: ……………………………..

School: …………………………………………

Please explain what evidence additional to this form you have taken into account, e.g. discussion with team leader, appraisal/performance review. Note how the evidence takes account of classroom performance. Set the teacher's performance in the overall context of the achievements of your school. Indicate whether, to the best of your knowledge, the information provided by the applicant is correct, that it derives from the applicant's own practice, and is representative of their overall performance.

Please make a final recommendation in the relevant box below. To be successful applicants must meet each of the standards.

Threshold Standards Met ☐

Not Yet Met ☐

Signed ……………………………………….. Date ……………………………………

Print name ……………………………………… School name ……………………………

EXAMPLE 2: A COMPLETED THRESHOLD ASSESSMENT APPLICATION FORM

IMPORTANT: PLEASE READ THE ENCLOSED GUIDANCE NOTES BEFORE STARTING TO COMPLETE THE APPLICATION FORM.

THIS APPLICATION FORM SHOULD BE HANDLED IN CONFIDENCE AT ALL TIMES.

Access to this form will be restricted to those who are playing a part in the assessment and verification process.

Personal Details

Surname: First Name(s):

Home Address/Telephone/e:mail/fax:

DfEE/Welsh Office Teacher Reference Number:

Career Details

Current post:

Date joined present school: Length in Post:

If not in school, current post and last teaching post (please give dates)

Subject or area specialism, if relevant:

Name and Location of School (or other employer):

Name of head:

Primary   Secondary   Other

Equal Opportunities Monitoring

The DfEE is committed to equal opportunities. We would like to monitor the profile of those applying for threshold assessment and the outcomes.

To enable us to do this, please complete the enclosed equal opportunities questionnaire and pass it to your headteacher who will forward it with your application form. The information you give us will be treated as confidential and will not form part of the application process.

Data Protection Act 1998

The Department for Education and Employment will process the information collected in this document for the purpose of assessing and monitoring teachers' applications to cross the performance threshold. This information will be processed only within the terms of the Department's Data Protection notification.

1. KNOWLEDGE AND UNDERSTANDING

Please summarise evidence that you:

- **have a thorough and up-to-date knowledge of the teaching of your subject(s) and take account of wider curriculum developments which are relevant to your work.**

I maintain a high level of fluency in French and I constantly update my knowledge of the language and culture, both essential in the teaching of my subject.
- Each year I visit France for a number of weeks and stay with a French family.
- I regularly read French newspapers, magazines and periodicals kept in the departmental files. These keep me up-to-date with topical issues and I use many articles with classes.
- I browse the Internet and download articles to use with the 6th Form, e.g. I have recently used an article and statistics concerning the death penalty in France and the USA when discussing capital punishment with Year 12 'AS' classes.
- I refer to the departmental library of publications on language teaching methodology *(available in Staff Room)*, and use ideas with my classes to help improve their oral fluency.

I use and have incorporated ICT into my teaching across the whole age range from 11 to 18 in order to improve and consolidate the listening skills and grammatical knowledge of pupils, encourage independent learning and increase motivation.
- I use the Internet to assist 'A' level coursework.
- I have used text manipulation software ('Fun with Texts') with the 2nd (Year 8) to 4th year (Year 10) this year and with the 1st (Year 7) to 4th year (Year 10) last year.
- I use CD ROM software ('French Grammar Studio') with years 8 to 13.
- I use the 'Virtual Language Laboratory' with years 12 and 13.
- I have used 'Pin Point' with year 8 this year.
- I attended a one-day course this year at Salford concerning how to use ICT effectively to raise standards in MFL. I have shared the information with my colleagues and put this into practice in my lessons.

(Records in the ICT department confirm the above.)

I am aware of the national strategies of literacy and numeracy and have incorporated them into my teaching.
- I encourage students to look at how language functions. With all years, I reinforce semantics and a knowledge of grammatical terms, e.g. Year 12 have analysed articles, classing words into grammatical categories *(see portfolio)*.
- With all years, I emphasise the importance of spelling and punctuation, (exercise books/tests), and discuss etymology, false friends etc.
- I encourage personal research using a dictionary, explaining its use, terminology etc. *(worksheets in portfolio)*.
- I use many number games and quizzes which consolidate vocabulary and encourage mental agility e.g. Yrs 10–13 play the TV game 'Countdown'.
- I introduce French money, speak of exchange rates (Year 8); students add up bills when acting out scenes at the café, shops etc.

I have kept up to date with curriculum changes including Curriculum 2000 post 16.
- I have participated in discussions concerning the new MFL curriculum.
- I have attended twilight sessions concerning Curriculum 2000.
- I have updated the Year 7 scheme of work *(available for inspection)* during 1999. The department and I have put this into practice.

Assessment by headteacher, noting any areas for further development.

Standard Met/Not Yet Met

2. TEACHING AND ASSESSMENT

Please summarise evidence that you consistently and effectively:

• plan lessons and sequences of lessons to meet pupils' individual learning needs

My files show that I plan lessons and sequences of lessons effectively to meet the needs of each whole group and the individuals within each group.

- I use extension tasks for the most able and for those pupils with an extensive previous knowledge of French. I have used (during 1998–99) separate workbooks for Year 7 pupils with 2/3 years' knowledge. (Copies in departmental files.)
- I formulated a separate programme of study for two Year 11 students preparing for 'AS' level who achieved a grade 'A'. (1998–99).
- I have produced separate worksheets/tests for a Year 11 student with dyslexia (1997–98) who achieved a 'C' GCSE.
- I have differentiated within my set 4 GCSE group (1999–00), setting different tasks/worksheets/tests to meet the needs of those pupils of lower ability and to raise their self-confidence in the subject.

I communicate learning objectives clearly to pupils.

- I give the pupils a summary of what they are to learn during the course of the lesson/sequence of lessons at the start of the lesson/sequence.
- At the end of the lesson, I give a résumé of what has been achieved or ask pupils to do this for the class. This gives my pupils a clear sense of progression in their learning.

I make effective use of homework and other learning opportunities.

- I regularly set and mark appropriate homework tasks (see lesson plans, pupils' books and colleagues' observation sheets), to allow pupils to review/consolidate classwork at their own pace.
- I feed back to pupils detailed information in their books based on departmental policy (SoW and exercise books), coupled with individual and personal guidance for improvement.
- I make use of opportunities for learning outside of the classroom by setting personal research for groups – Year 13 coursework, Year 7 research into various aspects of French life (1999).

• use a range of appropriate strategies for teaching and classroom management

I employ a full range of teaching methods to enthuse and motivate pupils.

- I exploit whole class question/answer work, pair-work, group work, ICT the internet, flashcards, OHP, audio/video resources, drama, quizzes, grammar explanation as tools in the learning process (see lesson plans, SoW, colleague observation sheets).

I have a sound and up-to-date knowledge of good teaching practices and techniques and how to enthuse pupils with a love of French and learning in general and have put these ideas into practice.

- I have read a number of recent publications (and watched videos) concerning good teaching practice and new ideas. (e.g. *Accelerated Learning in the Classroom* by Alistair Smith, *Closing the Learning Gap* by Mike Hughes, *Succeeding with Difficult Pupils* by Lee Cantor, training videos by Bill Rogers.)
- I refer to the Departmental library (Staff Room) regarding language teaching methodology.
- I have experimented with using music (Year 11) and mind-map techniques (Years 9–11) in my classroom to encourage learning. (I have discussed this with my Head of Department.)
- I involve the 'assistante' in team lessons (Years 8 and 12 during 1999/2000), which encourages interest and shows the pupils the true communicative nature of language.

I always encourage and support pupils by giving positive feedback at all times.

- Verbally in the classroom I praise, and raise pupils' self-esteem and confidence by the 'very good rapport I establish with them' (see observation sheets).
- I 'expect and attain high levels of behaviour and concentration', and I maintain discipline in a quiet, effective way – due to the 'obviously very good relationship' that I build with classes (observation sheets).
- I encourage motivation by displaying good examples of pupils' work on the walls in my classroom, which I utilise to the maximum effect with posters and prompts in French
- I use personally created stickers in the books of pupils to encourage motivation and create a sense of pride in their work (see exercise books).

I am aware of the semiotics of the classroom environment and its influence on learning and I use this as a positive learning tool.

- I arrange the seating in such a way that a variety of learning experiences can be easily accessed.
- I utilise my classroom walls to the maximum with bright posters and pupils' work.
- I believe the way a teacher dresses sets a tone and atmosphere and I always dress in a smart and business-like fashion.

2. TEACHING AND ASSESSMENT (continued)

Please summarise evidence that you consistently and effectively

- **use information about prior attainment to set well-grounded expectations for pupils and monitor progress to give clear and constructive feedback.**

I always use my knowledge of pupils' individual learning needs to plan lessons and sequences of lessons.

- Departmental record book, school records, unit test scores (produced for each pupil approximately every five weeks), homework and weekly test scores (recorded in my mark book), provide me with a large store of information on which to base my lesson planning and enable me to set targets for pupils.
- I ask pupils to complete individual self-assessment sheets once a year (in files) in which they write targets for improvement and which I monitor.
- I give individual oral assessments to all pupils from Year 9–13 (results in departmental record book), which enable me to monitor the progress my pupils have made and target individual needs for future improvement.
- I discuss with colleagues in the department pupils' abilities, progress and attitude as they are transferred so that I can prepare suitable plans and targets, and be aware of group dynamics.

I report clearly and in detail to parents concerning the achievement of their child.

- I use the school reporting process as a vital tool to inform parents about the progress of their child, in addition to the feedback I provide on an ongoing basis verbally and through pupils' exercise books.
- I report verbally on student progress to parents on Parent/Teacher consultation evenings.

Assessment by headteacher, noting any areas for further development. Each of the three standards above must be met.

Standard Met/Not Yet Met

Effective Teachers in Secondary Schools

3. PUPIL PROGRESS

Please summarise evidence that **as a result of your teaching your pupils achieve well relative to their prior attainment, making progress as good or better than similar pupils nationally. This should be shown in marks or grades in any relevant national tests or examinations, or school based assessment for pupils where national tests and examinations are not taken.**

❖ **Class example 1: Year 11 French group (set 4 of 4) who took their GCSE in 1998.**
- **Baseline:** I took the class on at the beginning of Year 11. Their average SAT level at KS3 was 5.9 and the average examination result at the end of Year 10 was 47%.
- **Actual progress:** Out of 21 pupils I taught, 18 had a positive residual in French. This means that 18 out of the 21 pupils I taught achieved better grades in the school with me than they did on average in other subjects.
- **Evaluation of progress:** The group had an overall average substantial positive residual of 0.66. The total group residual was 113.81. Again this effectively means that my French class of pupils had a value-added effect through my teaching of nearly 14 GCSE grades compared to how they did in other subjects in the school at GCSE. One of the pupils I taught had a positive residual of 12.52 (over 2.5 GCSE grades improvement on what they got in other GCSE examinations) and another 12.32.

❖ **Class example 2: Year 11 French group (set 1 of 4) who took their GCSE in 1999.**
- **Baseline:** I took the class on at the beginning of Year 10. The group had teacher assessed NC levels averaging 6 and SAT levels averaging 7.
- **Actual progress:** All 30 pupils I taught achieved a positive residual. All 30 pupils got a better grade in French than they did on average in other GCSE subjects.
- **Evaluation of progress:** The group had an overall average substantial positive residual of 1.12. This is equivalent to over one grade higher in French at GCSE than in other GCSE subjects. The total group residual was 133.49. Again this effectively means that my French class of pupils had a value-added effect through my teaching of over 33 GCSE grades compared to how they did in other subjects in the school at GCSE. Of the 30 pupils 27 gained an A* and 3 gained an A in French.

According to the PANDA report, the school's overall GCSE results were very high in comparison with schools nationally and with other similar schools in the county. Pupils in both my groups achieved, on average, better in French than in other subjects in the school. Therefore, my classes score well above average and my results are very favourable. County records show that my classes score above those of similar schools in North Yorkshire. *(See HoD.)*

❖ **Class example 3: 'A' level French group who took their 'A' level in 1999. (This group was taught by myself and one other teacher.)**
- **Baseline:** I took the group from the beginning of Year 12. Out of 11 pupils, 2 had an average GCSE score of 7.2 or more; 5 averaged 6.5–7.1; 4 averaged 6-6.4.
- **Actual progress:** Of the 11 students taught, 3 achieved a top A grade, 4 got a B, 2 got a C and 2 got a D.
- **Evaluation of progress:** 7 of the students achieved 'A' level grades which were above the grades their GCSE points score suggested. Their total value added 'A' level points score was 9 (equivalent to 4.5 'A' level grades of improvement between the 7 students). 2 of the students achieved 'A' level grades in complete agreement with what was predicted at GCSE. The other 2 students were just below the 'A' level grades predicted from GCSE. From the whole group I had a net value added figure of 5.75. Again this is equivalent to a total of nearly three 'A' level grades for the whole group.

❖ **Class example 4: Year 9 French group 1998–99 (set 3 of 4).**
- **Baseline:** A group of 27 students who, at the end of Year 8, were all working at teacher assessed levels of 4 or 5.
- **Actual progress:** All students achieved TA level 5 at the end of the year and the set average was 60%.
- **Evaluation of progress:** All pupils achieved the level targeted by departmental policy and the average class percentage was well in line with that of the other Year 9 sets.

(Analysis of all the statistics above is available in my portfolio.)

Assessment by headteacher, noting any areas for further development.

Standard Met/Not Yet Met

4. WIDER PROFESSIONAL EFFECTIVENESS

Please summarise evidence that you:

- **take responsibility for your professional development and use the outcomes to improve your teaching and pupils' learning**

I take a pro-active approach to my own learning and effectiveness as a classroom teacher.
- I maintain and improve my fluency by my annual visit to France – the best source of development for an MFL teacher. This enables me to provide a stimulating, target language environment for my pupils; it gives myself and them up-to-date knowledge of the language and culture and increases proficiency, understanding and interest.
- I accompany visits to MFL "A" level conferences (Updates 1998/99) which support the syllabus, widen my knowledge and that of my students.
- I am developing my ICT skill, which is an area where I am largely self-taught. I attended a one-day course (see section 1) and records in the ICT department show that I regularly put my knowledge into use to help reinforce grammar, improve listening skills, etc. (see section 1).

I am committed to my personal and professional development in education.
- During 1998/99, I shadowed colleagues in the Lower School, enabling me to be aware of the impact of the KS2 curriculum on the work carried out at KS3 and beyond, and to help pupils in the transition process from primary school.
- In 1999, I was successful in my application for the position of Deputy Head of Upper School and Work Experience Co-ordinator. My closer involvement with pupils and parents on a pastoral level has made me more aware of each pupil as an individual, and of the issues outside of school which can affect the learning of pupils in the classroom.
- I attended a 1-day course (1/2/00) concerning "Supporting Students with Eating Disorders" and a course (3/11/99) relating to "Drug and Alcohol Awareness". These have heightened my own awareness of problems which may affect students, and have enabled me to deal more effectively with these problems when they have arisen, and to support the students involved.
- I attended a Health and Safety Awareness day (24/4/99), and am qualified to make KS4 work experience placement visits – an important aspect of my new role as Work Experience Co-ordinator.
- I contributed to the criteria agreed upon for pupils in Year 11 to be mentored, and have been a mentor for two years. I believe this additional support has made significant differences to the students' potential examination outcomes.

- **make an active contribution to the policies and aspirations of your school.**

I consider that I make a valuable contribution to the school through my work as Deputy Head of Upper School.
- I am a representative for the school in my work with parents, with the ESWO and other outside agencies.
- I contribute to the ethos of the school by implementing a set of guidelines for pupils which will influence their behaviour and conduct in school, whilst lending support and advice where appropriate (as the Head of Upper School and colleagues will confirm). I encourage care and consideration for others and a pride in their own appearance.

I implement school policy and make a valuable contribution by co-ordinating the Work Experience programme.
- I ensure that all pupils receive a suitable placement from which they gain immense value and develop many key skills and interests.
- I represent the school in my dealings with the local community, industry and commerce.
- I organised an information evening for parents dealing with the aims and the process of the Work Experience programme.

I contributed to the departmental observation scheme.
- I was observed on 4 occasions and went into the classrooms of 4 colleagues. This enabled me to witness and to share examples of good classroom practice and participate in raising standards in support of school policy.

I am supportive of all aspects of school life.
- I have always been actively involved in Charity Week activities.
- I have helped at school drama productions (make-up, refreshments, etc.).
- I have accompanied the French exchange group on their journey from France.

Assessment by headteacher, noting any areas for further development. Both standards must be met.

Standards Met/Not Yet Met

Effective Teachers in Secondary Schools

5. PROFESSIONAL CHARACTERISTICS

Much of what you have said earlier in this form will give information about the professional characteristics you show in your teaching. Please give any further examples here of how you:

- ## challenge and support all pupils to do their best through

  inspiring trust and confidence
  building team commitment
  engaging and motivating pupils
  analytical thinking
  positive action to improve the quality of pupils' learning.

I believe I inspire trust and confidence, which enables pupils to work in a secure environment, and teachers and parents to have faith in my professional approach.
- I set high standards for pupils in my work as a classroom teacher, as Deputy Head of Upper School and W.E. co-ordinator.
- Colleagues and pupils view me as an optimistic, cheerful and positive person and one who is also approachable, sensitive and supportive.
- I give pupils the freedom and confidence to learn by creating a well-structured and caring classroom environment, where there is a "co-operative, pleasant atmosphere" (colleagues' observation).
- I expect and attain high standards of discipline and behaviour. Colleagues have observed that the "good behaviour and concentration come from the obviously excellent rapport built up".
- Feedback from parents (Parent/teacher consultation evenings), pupils and colleagues (observation) has always been positive.

I build a team commitment (with colleagues and pupils).
- I do this through my work as Deputy Head of Upper School and W.E. co-ordinator where I work closely with and am supportive of the Head of Upper School, form tutors, classroom teachers and pupils.
- I also do this through my general classroom approach, where I emphasise the need for each individual to contribute to the examples of good practice/new ideas with them and we form a united and happy team.

I use a variety of techniques and approaches to stimulate interest and to motivate the full range of abilities.
- I relate learning to everyday experience, e.g. comparing the lives of young French people with my pupils' lives.
- I give opportunities to use song, drama, games, quizzes, audio/video, personal presentation etc. (see section 1). e.g. Year 9 have presented TV weather forecasts which I videoed, Year 8 invented playlets about French family life.
- I introduced a system of reward certificates, which the department and I use to motivate.

I am aware of the need to use analytical thinking to improve my teaching.
- I have a deep interest in looking at the most effective methods of classroom management (e.g. see books in section 1). I have targeted the underachievement of boys in my Year 8 class. I re-arranged the seating, set them short-term learning targets, and used positive reinforcement and praise. Test results, homework, concentration in class demonstrate some improvement in learning.
- I organise lessons where possible into 'bite-size' pieces, changing activity every 10–15 minutes to improve concentration.
- At the end of each unit, I review my lessons, note the more/less successful aspects, and use these notes to improve planning.

I am constantly looking for ways to improve my effectiveness and thus the pupils' learning.
- I am increasing my own capabilities in my use of ICT in order to use it as another effective learning tool and to stimulate interest.
- I provide more opportunities for pupils to work as independent learners (readers in Years 7–9, CD-ROMs, personal research).

Assessment by headteacher, taking account of each aspect above and noting any areas for further development.

Standard Met/Not Yet Met

Declaration by applicant

I certify that I am eligible for assessment and that the information in this form is correct. I would like the evidence I have presented to be taken into account in assessing my work against the threshold standards. I understand that further pay progression on the upper pay range will be awarded on the basis of performance and accept that my annual reviews will be used to inform such judgements.

Signed .... Date ....

Declaration by headteacher (or equivalent if not in school)

Applicant name: ……………………………..

School: …………………………………………

Please explain what evidence additional to this form you have taken into account, e.g. discussion with team leader, appraisal/performance review. Note how the evidence takes account of classroom performance. Set the teacher's performance in the overall context of the achievements of your school. Indicate whether, to the best of your knowledge, the information provided by the applicant is correct, that it derives from the applicant's own practice, and is representative of their overall performance.

Please make a final recommendation in the relevant box below. To be successful applicants must meet each of the standards.

Threshold Standards Met   ❑

Not Yet Met   ❑

Signed ……………………………………………….   Date ……………………………………….

Print name ……………………………………………   School name ……………………………..

Appendix 17: OFSTED-style forms

1. Evidence form

Inspector's OIN			School URN		Observation type		L A D O
Year group(s)			Grouping	A M G S B O	Present/NOR		
Subject codes			Accreditation	GC AL AS VA VI VF VP VO XO	Observation time		
Teacher's status	QUTSN		Lesson type	CL GR IN MI XO	Support teacher/staff		
Teacher's code			Insp's EF No.		SIS Input Ref. No.		

Context

Evidence

When recording grades, use 0 to 7 to reflect judgements in the text on: Teaching; Learning; Attainment; Attitudes and behaviour:

Teaching		Learning		Attainment		Attitudes and behaviour	

2. Lesson observation aid

Context

Briefly describe the lesson and what pupils are doing.

Evidence

Record the evidence you have collected and your judgements made on the basis of that evidence.

Use evaluative words carefully to distinguish, for example, between very good and good, so that someone else would arrive at the same grade and evaluation:

1 = **excellent**

2 = **very good**

3 = **good**

4 = **satisfactory**

5 = **unsatisfactory**

6 = **poor**

7 = **very poor**

0 = **no evidence.**

Synonyms allow for varied, more interesting writing – for example:

▸ excellent = outstanding, superb

▸ satisfactory = competent, acceptable

and so forth.

Focus on strengths and weaknesses of the lesson and indicate what makes them strengths or weaknesses.

Give illustrations that you can draw on for examples of strengths and weaknesses when giving feedback on the lesson.

Give clear judgements, in accordance with the criteria in the OFSTED Handbook, especially on Teaching, Learning, Attainments and Attitudes and behaviour. Write in notes or in continuous prose.

Use all relevant criteria for which you have evidence.

Bibliography

Attwood, Tony (1988) *Raising Grades at GCSE*. Northants.: First and Best Publications.

Hughes, Mike (1999) *Closing the Learning Gap*. Stafford: Network Educational Press.

Robbins, Anthony (1986) *Unlimited Power*. London: Simon and Schuster.

Watkins, Chris (2000) *Managing Classroom Behaviour* – From Research To Diagnosis. London: Institute of Education with the Association of Teachers and Lecturers.

Covey, Stephen R. (1989) *The Seven Habits of Highly Effective People*. London: Simon and Schuster.

HH Dalai Lama & Howard Cutler (1998) *The Art of Happiness*. London: Coronet.

Powell, Robert (1997) *Raising Achievement and Active Whole Class Teaching*. Stafford: Robert Powell Publications.

Goleman, Daniel (1996) *Emotional Intelligence*. London: Bloomsbury Publishing.

DfEE Teaching Training Agency (1998) *National Standards for Headteachers*. HMSO.

DfEE (2000) *A Model of Teacher Effectiveness*. Report by Hay McBer to the Department for Education and Employment, June 2000. HMSO.